Black Boychik

The hilarious true story of a fat, mixed-race Jew crack addict who somehow becomes a comedian. Go Figure.

Sarge

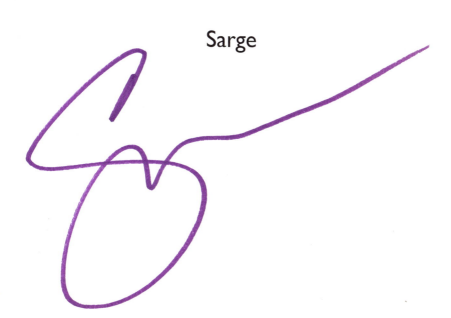

ISISBNBN 978-0-9962000-5-9

The author would like to thank Fran and Chet Pickman, Ania Pickman, Samuel Bernstein, Ronald Shore, Mike Lobert, Jimmy Heyward, Phil Cory, Rick Corso, Barry Sacks, Jere Henderson Sr., Morris Levy, Paul Bollen, David Marciano, Garry K. Marshall, Heather Hall, Greg Wilson, George Bartlett, HW Shane, David Mitchell, Kenny Kiefer, Kate Sochacki, Mitch Rosenberg, Arthur Harris, Sandy Levine, George Veras, Bobby Yalen, Jordan Weiss, Steven Golden, Diego Torres, Austin Jones, Mike Moralez, Steve Lankau, Jan Ziemecki, The Star Center, and Dr. Lucy Miller

The events and actions of the people written about in this book are accurate to the best of the author's memory. Any errors are unintentional and may be retracted or redacted in future editions if the publisher believes them to be both incorrect and material.

ZANBOBAN PUBLISHING, INC. © 2017 ALL RIGHTS RESERVED

For my son Zander, my wife Ania, and my man Sam Brown

FOREWORD BY GARRY K. MARSHALL

I've known Sarge for only six years, but it seems like much longer because he never stops talking. I'm sorry. I kid. I'm also in comedy.

Sarge came to my attention while I was the Master of Ceremonies at an annual event that's dear to my heart, the New York High School Alumni Show. Instead of staying backstage, as I had for most of the acts that night in 2009, I found a seat in the audience to watch him work. I like to watch comics work live, in the house, not from the wings. I've worked with quite a few of the great ones over the years, Jackie Gleason, Robin Williams, Louie CK, and let me tell you, Sarge really killed that night. His set was funny and touching, and he played great piano to top it off. I didn't say, "I like this guy," I said, "I can make money off this guy."

Sarge then went on my list of artists to use in my movies and work.

Comedians, the truly great ones, always find a way to draw humor and hilarity out of adverse circumstances. I had no idea then what Sarge's life was like before that night. We've come to know each other, from his work with me on my movie *New Year's Eve* to our many *kibitzing* sessions, seeing him perform again on DVDs, and listening to his comedy CDs.

Adopted, bi-racial, and overweight, not to mention a grown man with freckles, it's impossible to imagine that he could really be anything else other than a comedian. After all, God likes a good laugh too. But once you dig in to the book, and you read Sarge's real story, you will come to know that he is so much more than a comic with a great routine or an artist at the piano.

He's a noble human being and a true friend. I've come to admire the father that Sarge is to his son Zander, the husband that he is to his wife Ania, and the son that he is to his parents. All hats that I myself wear. The biggest hat I wear these days is Grandpa. I assume someday he'll do that pretty well too.

Anyway, I recommend you read the book and discover Sarge's journey—it may make your own journey easier and for sure it'll make you laugh. That's a lot for me to say about a man whose real name I don't know and don't care to know. Enjoy "Sarge." I have and still do.

Garry K. Marshall
Los Angeles, California

PREFACE

To My Dear Little Man Zander,

My gorgeous son...While I'm writing this letter, you're running around the house at one in the afternoon humming and playing and full of energy. JOY. Total and complete joy. (Wow, I just got a bit choked up writing that.) This is for you, my son. You're six years-old at the time I'm writing this, and I'm fifty-three. Because of my newly felt sense of impending mortality, I feel more than compelled to tell you as much as I possibly can about living a happy, successful, dutiful, God-based, free from organized religion, gambling, drugs, or alcohol, honest-to-the-best-of-my-ability LIFE.

I hope with all my heart that you won't make the same mistakes I've made.

But if you do make these mistakes, or if you already have by the time you read this, or if you are about to make some mistakes that are totally, uniquely yours—at least this book can serve as your roadmap home. Like just about all Dads, I want you to have more than I had, but that doesn't mean money, or things. To me it means a relationship with your father—the man I really am to you—so you can keep that forever. Because I love you more than anything I've ever known, and that love surprised me. I love you because you have my smile, my teeth, my cheeks; because you're from your beautiful Mom; because of your irascibility—you should have a dictionary downloaded in your smartphone handy while you read this—or in whatever amazing new technology exists by then—so Daddy doesn't have to edit himself, 'cause as you've already found out from being my son, I'm long winded and have a hard time editing myself—I love you because of your curly hair; I love you because you ARE, just because you exist, and I always will. Whoever and whatever you grow into being, I want you to have this book as a reference into what made me ME, and how maybe that has had a hand in making you YOU.

For my son. That's as good a reason as there is to do anything in this world. But along with that, I'm writing this so I don't have to continually bore you by telling these stories over and over as you grow up—sitting on the porch, getting old, boring you, boring the kids you'll someday bring over to visit, and boring myself. For some strange reason I'm terrified of becoming Grandpa (I mean MY father, I can't write about Mommy's father without getting into trouble with her. So let her write her own book. In Polish,) Mainly, I don't want to become your Grandpa Chet in one really annoying way: He repeats over and over and over and OVER the same *faux-poignant* anecdotal stories without endings, or relevance, from the 1930s or whenever, just to hear his own voice. They always start, "Wait till you hear this, this is FUNNY." And they never are. I'm sorry Dad, but as interesting as your life may or may not have been, the storytelling gene skipped a generation. Of course, I'm adopted, so I don't know whether your own father was a storyteller, nor do I know if either of my biological parents were (or are). But I do know that somewhere, somehow, a generation was skipped.

Zander, these are some of the things I want you to know about:

How I was born and adopted by two people who pretended I was someone else—namely a little white boy.

How I could play piano by ear at six years-old.

How Grandma and Grandpa were impossible to live with when they were MY Mommy and Daddy.

How I was shipped off to boarding school in Connecticut at age twelve, got into two prestigious universities—and finished at neither one.

How I got hired and spent the mid-80s working at two world-famous modeling agencies in New York, was accepted to the Lee Strasberg Theater Institute, got hired at four major television networks and was fired from them all.

How I got addicted to doing tons of drugs and alcohol, resulting in a year of homelessness.

How I had one friend left in my life who helped me get to treatment where I prayed just one prayer on one night and it all turned around.

How through the grace of the universe, you will never have to go without anything you need—because I am here now, and you will never see your Daddy high or drunk.

Finally… I'm writing this because I'm blessed with the gift of addiction. I say gift because had I not hit bottom; had I not discovered, acknowledged, and accepted these things about myself—I would never have met your mother. And even if I had, I don't believe I would have been much of a husband, let alone a father. Maybe you will grow up to have some of my issues—severe A.D.D. and a touch of obsessive compulsive disorder, with a compulsion for gambling. Sure, there are medications for some of these things, but that's not always enough. By NOT partaking in any of these addictions, I have a continued shot at a life which many of us who are so afflicted believe to be beyond our wildest dreams. You're the biggest part of that being true. It's a lot of pressure for a little guy but I see your life as a gift of my sobriety and abstinence from these things, and hopefully it gives you a Dad who's loving, kind, gentle and attentive to you and your Mommy's needs.

This was unimaginable seventeen years before you were born.
I'm FIFTY THREE.

That's the first time I've seen fifty-three in writing as it pertains to ME! Kinda like when you're still writing 2016 on checks a full two months into 2017. Oh—checks. Only people about fifty years-old remember checks, and only people close to a HUNDRED and fifty still write them at the supermarket—on the ten items or less line.

I used to think that the most amazing fact of my life was that I was once fatally addicted to PCP and crack and alcohol. I used to think that I was alive (by the grace of God) because I was supposed to write the *Absolutely amazing story of how I got clean, got my life together, and miraculously rejoined the cast of my hit network sitcom.* I used to think. I used to think a lot of things. But as of this writing, there is no hit sitcom. No great wealth. No story of a fall from grace that leads inevitably, momentously to great stardom. Whatever. NOW I think real life has been enough. It IS enough. More than enough. It's amazing. All the stories I can remember; the places I've been and things I've done; the stages I entertained on; the marriage before I met your gorgeous Mom, who I love and adore—not the least of which because she gave you to me...

Okay, if I'm honest, there's one exception to all this stuff about giving up the fantasy of what my life was supposed to be, and embracing my real life. That exception is Oprah Winfrey, and the last vestiges of my crazy dream of going on her show (that isn't on the air anymore) and being selected for her book club. That would have been AWESOME. (Zander, in case, by some Act of God, Oprah is no longer the most admired woman on the planet by the time you read this, she was someone who came from nothing and became EVERYTHING. She started schools in Africa, yo-yo dieted, was more famous than any President, had a talk show, helped lots of people, had her own magazine and put herself on the cover every month, and was generally a brilliant force of nature.) Anyway. Though Oprah gave up her show and her book club, and I'll never get to tout my book with her, I still catch myself having that daydream—the one where Oprah slides forward in her comfy chair, with her perfectly manicured hands, and asks me in stunned amazement, "Is that really true? You didn't actually know you're Black until you were forty years old? You were once a crack addict and homeless? And now you're rich, famous, and thin! How amazing! How inspiring! Everyone in the audience is going home with a copy of your book! And a new car! And a house!" She did stuff like that.

But yes, Zander, it IS true that I didn't know for sure that I'm half Black until I was forty. So you, my son, are 25% Black, 25% Russian

Jew, 50% Polish Catholic, and 100% American—which comes out to 200%, so now you know why I always sent you to Mommy with your math homework. But, my Oprah daydream notwithstanding, I want you to know all of the stories of my life, in my words. I want you to know my thoughts, and know my perspective, so you can form your very own.

Sometimes life is short. I have this chance to tell you my story, but not everyone does. I had a BFF named Sam Brown who left long before he should have, and he never got to do this. Sam helped your Daddy become a comedian, and that gift has paid for everything we have and ever will have. Losing him was so painful, but it also made me an even better Dad and comedian. I want you to know about me and my life before you—but I also want you to know about Sam, so you can be grateful to him for his gift to us. He gave me my life, and so, in turn, that means he also had a huge part in giving you your life.

I love you pal, and always will. Enjoy every day. Love everyone and everything, infinitely. Forgive people easily and hold no grudges, so you can have the happiest life possible.

Love always,
Your Daddy, forever, Sarge

A BABKA BABY BOY IS BORN

It was 1961. Whites and Blacks were still drinking from separate water fountains. The civil rights movement hadn't picked up steam yet, and a young college girl from an orthodox Jewish family *hooked-up* with a Black man. She became pregnant and fled her native Chicago to have the baby in Florida. I'm sure she had another option available to her, but for some reason, which I've never been able to ascertain, and am overjoyed she didn't explore, she went through with the pregnancy. So she flew to Miami Beach and checked in to the Betsy Ross Motel on Collins. I don't know where she got the money, but I'm thrilled that she got the inclination. She planned to give the baby up for adoption with the proviso that he or she be adopted by a Jewish couple. I've also learned she was *heavy-set*, polite for *obese*, so I guess she had already been *showing* prior to *showing*. White America had not officially decided to make friends with Black America, and Orthodox Jew America was its own universe. I can't begin to imagine how impossibly difficult it would have been for my biological mother to go to her family or friends and tell them she'd *shtupped* a Black Gentile. Thank God she bravely went ahead with it. With me.

Mt. Sinai Hospital, on Alton Road, in Miami Beach, Florida: I was born "Baby Boy" and later named Steven Charles Pickman by my adoptive parents. Nine pounds and change. A big boy. My adoptive grandfather Poppy Herman was a fan of both boxing and wrestling and instantly nicknamed me "Primo," after the behemoth failed boxer turned professional wrestler Primo Carnera. When Poppy would send me postcards from Tucson, Arizona or Miami Beach he would address them "My Primo."

Today, Miami Beach is SOBE—South Beach—a destination for wannabes, Cubans, the South American rich, Euro-trash, model chasers, and people making weekly pilgrimages to cruise ships so they can wear speedos and eat like they have two asses. But back in the early '60s, Miami Beach was one of the coolest places on Earth, for different reasons. It was part of the show business circuit of Las Vegas, Los Angeles, the Catskills (also known as the Borscht Belt), and New York City. Miami Beach was also the prime vacation destination for New York Jews, and it was their favorite place to kvetch. (Kvetching— a Yiddish word for complaining—is a central characteristic of Jewish people; chronic complainers who are genetically predetermined to suffer from terminal dissatisfaction. Old joke: A waiter comes over to a table of Jews eating and sarcastically asks, "Is ANYTHING alright at this table?") Everyone who was anyone went to Miami Beach, staying at the Fontainebleau, the Eden Roc, Roney Plaza, the Saxony... Celebrities, politicians, musicians, writers, millionaires, rabbis, conmen, restauranteurs, and retirees.

It was into this world that a White Jewish couple adopted a young White Jewish single mother's baby. No one told them anything about the father. I was very light skinned. Maybe my adoptive parents saw me and suspected something, but let denial clamp down and shove that thought far, far away. Maybe they were just stupid. But neither of them said a word, not then, not EVER, until I brought up the subject of me looking Colored. That was what we were called then: Colored. Later on, we were Afro-Americans, then Blacks, now African-Americans, which strikes me as odd, because people in Nigeria don't call themselves African-Africans. Beyond being Colored, in 1961, though, if my mixed parentage had been acknowledged, I would have also been called Mulatto—a term that has all but disappeared today, along with its ugly stepchildren, Quadroon and Octoroon.

For years in my comedy act I said I was Mocha. Now I call myself Beige. Both words get a laugh. They are playful and funny, but also very neutral, with no troublesome racial overtones.

My adoptive parents lived in Great Neck, Long Island. Were it not for a certain gentleman's love of Jewish babka, we might never have met. Enter my HERO, my grandfather. I called him Poppy. His name was Herman W. Shane, and he was a successful business man and a fixture at the Friars Club in New York. (The Friars Club today is known for irreverent, vulgar roasts hosted by Jeff Ross on Comedy Central, where comedians take shots at pop icons like Donald Trump, Roseanne, Flavor Flav, and Mike Tyson. Back in Poppy's day, though, it was a closed fraternity of show business people.)

Poppy's daughter Fran had a terrible problem: she couldn't conceive. No in vitro then. No surrogacy. Adoption was the only option.

Then as now, it isn't WHAT you know, it's WHO you know. Poppy had a lifelong pal and Friar brother named Dr. Harry Kraff who happened to have become the world renowned Chief of OB-GYN at Mt. Sinai Hospital in Miami Beach. Poppy was in New York, making the twenty-block walk home from his office in the RKO building, and he couldn't stop thinking about his daughter's predicament. Suddenly he got an idea. He stepped over to a pay phone and called his dear friend Dr. Harry. Over the very expensive long distance call (that in those days probably cost a quarter) Poppy asked Harry if he could help track down a baby for his daughter to adopt. "Where are you?" Dr. Harry asked. "What do you mean, where am I?" said Poppy. Harry wanted to know how close Poppy was to Ebinger's Bakery in Brooklyn. "You do me a favor, and I'll do you a favor," said Dr. Harry. "Go to Ebinger's and get me a chocolate babka, NO NUTS, and I'll find your daughter a baby."

Simple.

Poppy got in a cab and went to Brooklyn to Ebinger's. He took a number, waited in line, ordered not one but two chocolate babkas, NO NUTS, and had them boxed and tied up with string. He hopped another cab to La Guardia Airport, boarded a twenty-nine-dollar flight to Miami Beach. Babkas in hand, Poppy arrived at Mt. Sinai Hospital on Alton Road in Miami Beach, and delivered them directly to Dr. Harry. In turn, Dr. Harry took Poppy to the room of a young woman who was ready to deliver her baby, and told Poppy, "You're getting what she's having."

My adoptive parents, Poppy's daughter Fran and her husband Chet, flew down with Chet's parents in tow, and they adopted me. Fair trade. Babkas for a Baby Boy.

You can't write this shit!

Even though, I am, in fact, writing it.

They brought me home in a basket to Great Neck, a lily White upper class suburb of New York. Maybe they really didn't have a clue that they had adopted a half-Black baby. After all, Poppy had seen the mother with his own eyes: a heavyset White Jewish girl with red hair and freckles. Complicated, but thankfully for me, since, given the racial climate in 1961, formally acknowledging my mixed-race background would have made me unadoptable to Whites. Being unable to conceive can be emotionally overwhelming to couples. Maybe for Fran and Chet Pickman, their longing for a child was so deep, that subconsciously they just refused to see me—in all my true colors. However it happened, I'm one lucky dude. My Poppy traded two babkas for a nine pound, eight ounce black and white cookie.

The excitement of the new arrival had barely subsided, when a different kind of excitement took over. Right from the start, I had health complications—a condition that needed to be corrected surgically called pyloric stenosis, a disorder of the pyloric valve between the stomach and esophagus. This valve regulates the flow of food and liquid to the stomach, and if it spasms, feeding the baby is difficult and can be impossible. It was months of touch-and-go as to whether I'd make it, but a gifted surgeon named Dr. Bronster at Long Island Jewish Hospital did his thing, and eventually I was in the clear. I still have a little two inch scar on my belly from the procedure. Color-wise, I may not have been entirely pink, but after all the hospital visits and surgery, I think my new parents were so happy I was still alive, that I could have been green and they wouldn't have cared. Love is blind, right?

I wouldn't know for a fact that I'm half-Black until forty years later—in a cell phone conversation from the pool deck of Caesar's Palace in Las Vegas. (Many of the most important moments of my life have happened on pool decks nationwide.) I had started actively looking for my birth mother through a search service, and I got a call from Susan, my biological mother, and among other things, she confirmed that my biological father was, in fact, a Black man. She thought it was important to say, "We had a fling, NOT a relationship!"

Good to know.

What did I actually know and when did I know it?

All through my early childhood—in what became fertile ground for the makings of a comedian—the pointed question was always there, and always asked, by just about everyone: WHAT ARE YOU, ANYWAY? When I asked Mom and Dad, the only thing they would say is, "You're from people just like us."

Not helpful.

So my imagination ran amok. "I'm a Cuban Jew which makes me Cubish," I'd tell people, or, "I'm Nigerian Jewish, Ni-Jewian." I did whatever it took, sensing, if not actually understanding, that my answers were funny. By the time I did know the power of humor, the answers I would come up with to satisfy inquisitors got even wilder.

I had big lips, reddish, afro hair, and freckles, and I was traded for two babkas by a man who loved comedians. Poppy passed away fifteen years before I became a professional comic, but I'm a comedian today partly in tribute to him. I channel him in my pre-show preparations. I was his gift to my parents, and in every show I try to re-gift his love to the world. It all started with a couple of Brooklyn babkas. For me, babka is life. And it's very, very filling.

A JEW IN THE PROMISED LAND

By now, I've been able to learn from conversations with aunts, uncles, cousins, and school friends, that EVERYONE in my family knew I was racially different, everyone except ME. My parents specialized in denial and they still do.

Mid-to-late '60s: I remember fuzzy images of a draped coffin on the black and white Zenith in the corner of our apartment, and snippets of sad comments about someone called Dr. Martin Luther King. Was it really MLK? Or am I just mixing it up with JFK or RFK?

This is Douglas Edwards, from the steps of the Capitol, Washington, CBS News...

I have vague memories of events that changed the world, and their possible relation to me. But what's CRYSTAL CLEAR are the radio voices of Bob Murphy, Lindsey Nelson, and Ralph Kiner doing play-by-play of New York Mets games.

The Mets I remember.

My mother never misses a single Mets broadcast to this day and she's eighty years-old. Now she lives a block away from me in Florida, but she still never misses a chance to tell anyone who asks (and many who do not) that she used to live four blocks from Ebbets Field in Brooklyn on Bedford Avenue, home of the Brooklyn Dodgers, and two stoops down from Ralph Branca—the Dodgers pitcher who famously threw the pitch that the Giants' Bobby Thompson hit into the left field bleachers—*The Shot Heard Round the World*. The radio call by Russ Hodges of that home run is something that if you're even a casual fan, you've heard in countless documentaries, not to mention Ken Burns epic Baseball. It's etched in every fan's memory.

The Giants win the pennant, the Giants win the pennant, the Giants win the pennant!

Before I was born, my family ate, slept, dreamt, and bled Brooklyn Dodger blue. When the Dodgers left Brooklyn in 1957, they were

Horrified! Furious! Crestfallen! In 1962 the New York Mets arrived and all of that energy and emotion found a new focus. (Why the Yankees were never in contention warrants an entire book of its own.) My mother became a rabid Mets fan, and so I did too. There was no discussion. You live twenty minutes from the ballpark and that's who you root for, and I can honestly say that some of the most wonderful, safe, comfortable memories I have from childhood are those of the sound of a baseball broadcast playing in the kitchen.

I even remember the jingles of the Mets sponsors.

My beer is Rheingold, the dry beer, think of Rheingold whenever you BUY beer… It's refreshing not sweet, it's the extra dry treat, won't you try extra dry Rheingold beeeeeeeeeeeer. I can hear it like it was yesterday. *Today's game is also brought to you by your Tri-State Chrysler-Plymouth Dealers… and by First National City Bank… the only bank your family ever needs…*

We summered in Long Beach, Long Island. Obviously a beach town, but more importantly THE beach town on Long Island's south shore. Our rental house on Pacific Boulevard was across the street from the most amazing deep, sandy, rough ocean beach you'd ever seen. Pacific Beach was huge to me. The biggest expanse of sand dunes I could imagine.

That's why it was so shocking to see the pictures when hurricane Sandy hit Pacific beach and eroded and decimated my childhood haunt.

My Nanny and Poppy's place was right on the beach. As a kid, I couldn't wait to get over there. They had the whole top floor facing the ocean of Lido Gardens and this would be the scene of my first real comedy training.

Poppy and I would walk on the beach three jetties down and back and he would hold my hand. I remember my arm being stretched to its limit just to hold his hand. I had pain in my shoulder from it, but I didn't care, because it was Poppy's hand and he was my hero.

He would teach me jokes that he wanted me to learn and then

perform back at the pool deck in between his card games. I was stocky and my thighs would be chafed already one hundred feet into the walk. He'd take me in the ocean for a *dip* and the water was chaotic and swirling, rough and littered with huge green sheets of seaweed. He'd wade in to the turbulent water up to his shins and splash upward toward himself with his hands and he'd tell me to wait at the water's edge because, to say I wasn't much of a swimmer would have been an understatement. I didn't like to get my head wet (a phobia I wouldn't outgrow for several years).

But that was the least of my problems.

The salt water splashing up between my chubby thighs would hit the chafed area and, well, you know what I'm talking about. Shoulder pain, chafing pain.

What I wouldn't give to take just one more of those walks with Poppy today to tell him what all those jokes became in my life. They'd become a profession, a calling, an obsession.

He taught me jokes, asked me to do impressions, anything funny. Poppy loved to laugh, and he loved people who made people laugh. (His favorite comedian was Gene Baylos, a guy who kinda "never made it" but he always loved the underdog.)

Poppy laughed with his whole body. His face was bright like a brushfire and his man-boobs jiggled.

After our walk and dip, we'd head back to his card game on the pool desk. I'd sit right next to my Poppy, off to the corner near the cabanas. Old men sat at every table—shuffling, dealing, playing, spying on the others' cards, holding their hands behind them like they were under arrest, looking on expressionless, and smoking White Owl cigars—their man-boobs spilling out everywhere.

These men didn't work out, they *worked*.

Poppy's table was an all-star team of Jewish professionals. On any given weekend, at any spot at the table, it could be the Judge from the Bronx, the Dermatologist, Mink Silberman from Riverdale, and real comics too, from the Friars Club, giants like Milton Berle, Red Buttons, George Burns, Jackie Gayle, and Jackie Mason. It was like any scene from Garry Marshall's movie *Flamingo Kid*, based almost entirely on days like these. The corner of the table right next to my Poppy was where I sat in a beach chair seven times my size. My backstage area. I'd watch, with no idea of what was going on, just observing every move of the gin game. Sometimes it would seem like an eternity, and then, the muttering, and the caustic comments would be interrupted by one of them announcing proudly, "GIN!"

Someone had GIN!

My cue to go on with *STEVIE SHOWTIME!* Poppy would quiet the men gathered, point to me, and say, "Okay, GO!"

And GO I did. I'd start with an impression of the little girl from the Shake and Bake commercial, with a southern accent, I'd say "And I hayyyyllllped." Then I'd go into an impression of Tom Dooley, a TV pitch man urging people to move to Florida from the New York area (as though they needed a commercial for that) and I'd gesture with my arm, swiping it through the air like a tennis forehand smash "C'mon down!" (To Florida). The men would roar with laughter as though I'd just told the most hilarious joke. Even the comics from the Friars Club would laugh—though I'll never know if they truly thought I was funny, or if they were just being nice to Poppy's strange looking grandson out of respect.

Then the dermatologist with the biggest man-boobs of all, and a tongue clearly three times the size of the inside of his mouth, would wait for a space in the performance and he'd make his request, and it was ALWAYS the same request.

"Do the busy signal Stevie, do the busy signal!"

(For those of you not of a certain age, once upon a time if you called someone who was already talking to someone else on the phone, an intermittent buzzing noise would tell you that the phone was busy, and you would have to call back. No call-waiting then.)

I was only too happy to comply with the fat dermatologist's request. I'd put my whole body into it, contort my face as though in pain and, "Do the busy signal"—basically just make buzzing sounds and funny faces—and they'd ROAR. Then I'd finish with a knock-knock joke. "Knock, knock." "Who's there?" "Chaim." "Chaim, who?" I'd draw it out, making them wait for the most mediocre punchline in the history of punchlines, "Chaim telling you for the last time, my last name's not WHO?"

And the ROAR would come again.

All that beautiful laughter. Then as now, it isn't the quality of the material, but the quality of the comedian. And I looked like a cartoon—this adorable, articulate, chubby, mocha, miniature Catskill comic. They loved comedy, so they loved me.

I looked forward to those *shows*. I lived for them, not so different from the way I love to do shows now. The material's better I hope, the comedian is also hopefully better, but the reason for doing it is the same. The reaction. The positive, wonderful, thunderous reaction. The ROAR. It brings joy, it makes life worth living, and it makes everything else disappear. What a magical power it is, what a gift. Even at six years-old, I think I understood how vital it is to my being, like breathing. Poppy always tagged the laughter by telling *the audience*, his friends, "And you should hear him play the piano too, like a chubby Liberace ovah here!"

It was 1967, and comedy was no longer the only way I could make a spectacle of myself. Because earlier that summer, the MOMENT had happened after my parents took me to see *The Sound of Music* for my birthday.

When we came home from the show, I wandered over to the spinet piano in our house which I HAD NEVER TOUCHED prior to that MOMENT. I pulled out the bench, sat down, and opened the lid. I thought of the songs from the show, positioned my tiny little fingers on the keyboard, and began to play.

The sound came from the piano that sounded like the songs from the show.

I kept playing, all the songs that you walked out of the show humming because you can't get them out of your head. I was getting them FROM my head and playing them by ear the very first time I touched the piano. My parents came running from the bedroom and stood to my right, not saying anything, just standing in sheer amazement I guess.

From "Edelweiss" to "Climb Every Mountain," I played 'em all, and when I finally stopped, my mother said "Where did you learn that?" I said with the lisp that I had then "I don't know, but it's sssssssimple."

My mother immediately went to the phone and called her father, my hero, Poppy and told him of the MIRACLE, the GENIUS, the VAN CLIBURN right here amongst us. Maybe three days later I was in Manhattan at Julliard being evaluated. Six years-old and labeled by the Julliard people in terms I didn't understand.

He's a phenomenon, and he's a genius. Do you realize how few children, how few PEOPLE can play this way?

I didn't know what any of that meant, but I knew it was good.

After all, it made everyone pay attention to me.

My training began the following week. The plan was to send a professor to the house weekly until I was old enough to attend classes at Julliard. So each week Professor Judy Greenberg would come, and play a piece for me on the piano in our house, and supply me with the sheet music. Each week, I'd listen to her play it, and rather than try to read the music, I'd get my father to get a vinyl record of whatever song it was and play it for me on the phonograph. Then, I'd sit down at the piano and play it, ignoring the music that was on the music stand.

Each week, Judy would assign a song, and each week, I'd play it.

She thought I was learning the assignments.

It would later be discovered I wasn't learning any assignments. I was playing exclusively by ear. I could not read a note. I still can't. I would learn much later why my A.D.D. brain couldn't read music, and also couldn't do math. It wasn't that I was unwilling to try, or learn, I was learning disabled as it pertains to those two areas, music and math. We now know that music is very mathematical in its design and everything adds up. Not to me, but to normal people and in this way I'm not normal, THANK GOD, because like my multi-ethnicity, my abnormal brain has turned out to be a massive gift from God or the Universe. Whoever or whatever I should thank, I'm grateful. It has given me a profession and the ability to entertain people. Like an acrobat, or a contortionist, I share my beautiful flaw with the world every time I perform. Thank you God.

We were always with Poppy at the resort in the Catskill Mountains called Grossinger's—a riotously colorful world of kosher dining and non-stop entertainment. The hotel seemed to go on forever, with endless promenades and hallways and *secret* passageway shortcuts to various parts of the hotel.

The hallways I loved most were practically wallpapered with framed photos of famous entertainers in tuxedos, swimsuits, warm-up suits, evening gowns—all seemed to be taken by a photographer named *The Famous Weegee*. Weegee was a renowned New York photographer who chronicled crime, mob rub-outs, show biz, high society, city hall, and everything else that mattered in the city. His nickname was a nod to the Ouija board—a device that supposedly could tell the future in the same way that Weegee knew where to find *the scene of the crime* before even the police got there.

Everyone who was anyone played the Catskills, or if you were a politician or a mobster who wanted to make an impression, you showed up to press the flesh: Joan Rivers, Johnny Carson, Buddy Hackett, Sinatra, Sammy Davis Jr., Governor Nelson Rockefeller, Van Cliburn, Jascha Heifetz, Myron Cohen, Rodney Dangerfield, Norm Crosby, Jan Peerce, Buddy Lester, Shecky Green, Sophie Tucker, Eddie Fisher, Eddie Cantor, Red Buttons, Judy Garland, Alan King, the Everly

Brothers, the Smothers Brothers, the Ritz Brothers, the Nicholas Brothers, Dr. Joyce Brothers.

The Jewish Alps. The Borscht Belt.

It WAS the SHIT.

I'd walk along the framed photographs in the Grossinger's slowly, with my head tilted to the side to look at every picture, taking it all in like I was studying for a final exam. I was mesmerized by those photos, imagining myself up there with all of those glamorous people. Every time I was at Grossinger's, I couldn't wait until the adults were occupied eating, or napping, or *shvitzing* in the steam room, so I could lose myself in the walls of those halls.

Poppy arranged for a piano to be put in the busiest place in the whole hotel with Dave Geiver, (who was known as "Geiver the Slave Driver" for his maître d' style in the dining room) outside the doors to the dining room.

I would play the piano and invariably people would come over and ask to hear their favorites. "Can you play 'My Yiddishe Mama'?" I'd ask them to hum it, and that was my method of learning song after song. The problem comes in the fact that maybe one in one thousand Jews can hum a tune well enough so that you actually know what song they're humming. Marvin Hamlisch, Eddie Fisher, Irving Berlin—fantastic hummers. The rest of the Jews? Stay in the audience please, and DON'T HUM. But somehow, however off-key or vague, I'd sit at the Grossinger's piano and figure out how to play whatever people asked.

After a couple of stints, Geiver came out with a huge brandy snifter and put it on the piano. He put a dollar in it *from his own pocket,* apparently to get me started. And the quarters and dollars poured in, going in the snifter and back downstairs into the coin slots in the Grossinger's Pinball Arcade, feeding my nightly pinball binges. I still came out ahead, since bills couldn't go in the pinball games back then. The dollar bills, and occasional fives, went into my back pocket, where

I would carefully button them in. Some nights I could barely close that button. That was a gooooooood night.

The first real entertainer I ever saw was Don Rickles. Talk about a gooooooood night.

I was hidden down between Poppy's knees under the ringside table he always had at the Playhouse at Grossinger's. Hidden because children were not allowed to be in the massive one thousand-seat showroom. I watched Don Rickles DEMOLISH the crowd. People were pounding with their open hands, slapping the little round tables with the starched tablecloths, knocking over drinks with almost every comment he made—draped over each other, holding hands over hearts, screaming like they were having a massive heart attack. Rickles stomped around sweating and screaming, and the audience stomped and screamed even louder.

It was raucous, and amazing, and inspiring. It was *life*.

Of course, I had no idea at all what he was talking about.

But the crowd sure did, and I decided that night: *I wanna do what he's doing.*

For a long time after that, my corner of Poppy's card table at the pool deck would be the only way I could fulfill that dream. That night seeing Don Rickles for the first time and its life-changing impact wouldn't find full flower until twenty-three years later, in a place even more unlikely than a poolside card table. It would be on the beach—again, the beach—behind an addiction treatment center in Delray Beach, Florida.

But that was still a long way off.

DRAMA OF THE *GIFTED* CHILD

Early on I was labeled *gifted*. It wasn't just being able to play piano by ear at six. Even before that, by age three I was reading *Hardy Boys* novels. I guess it's true that I was gifted. *I was also weird*. My parents loved throwing around that *gifted* label. They put me in a *special* school with an accelerated curriculum—that cost double what a regular private school would have cost. Between that and the professor from Julliard, they had official confirmation of my *giftedness*, and could lord it over their friends and relatives, incessantly bragging about their *gifted* child.

That this may have been overcompensating a little on their part, trying to drown out the whispers about my dubious ethnic makeup and how different I looked from everyone else—and that maybe I could have a little compassion—well, that only occurred to me... about... five minutes ago.

I was so smart. I was so clueless.

So I was enrolled at the prestigious Sands Point Academy, where I would not prove to be as popular with my classmates as I was with a bunch of old Jews around a card table or at a Catskills resort playing piano.

To get to school, I had to endure a seventy-minute bus ride with children who were delighted to point out in ways that we would now term politically incorrect to the extreme, that I was not, in fact, White like them. It was my first recallable experience with out-and-out racism. I hated this bus ride. And the older high school kids on the bus were the cruelest. The worst were the Cohen brothers. Not Joel and Ethan. That would be *Coen*. Allen and Jay Cohen—the names have *not* been changed to protect the guilty. They were nasty grown-up rich kids that viciously led a barrage of racial jokes directed at me that are uncomfortable to even write about. Let's just say this, Cher's song "Half-Breed" was the biggest hit on the radio then, and the Cohen brothers played it at least three times on the way to school, getting everyone on the bus to sing along and call me *Half-Breed* right to my face. They also called me *Fat Albert*—the freckled, chubby nigger.

I hated taking the bus.

I remember one instance on the bus where they were trying to convince me that my mother was not my mother. Yes, I was adopted, but in the strange mixed-up logic of children, I never thought about my adoptive mother not being my mother. From that point forward, I made my Mom hide out of sight when the bus came up the block to pick me up in the morning.

The ride home wasn't as bad as the ride to school. My teenaged oppressors had sports practice, so my afternoons were easier to endure.

Here's the part I now understand that I wasn't aware of then: Racism is sheer ignorance. It's fear of the *Other*—mindless hate directed at anyone or anything that isn't like you. I had no knowledge of this. It was 1968. As a nation, Blacks and Whites had just begun to drink out of the same drinking fountains and eat at the same lunch counters. But I didn't know anything about that. I thought they all hated me for ME—not because of my race—which I still didn't quite see as different from theirs. I mean, I *understood*, I just didn't *understand*. I personalized their hatred, the jeering, the spit being flung in my hair, and I became deeply ashamed of myself.

There was something *horribly* wrong with me. *Gifted?* I was *shameful.* And I would carry this shame around for many, many more years… Decades.

The faces of those kids are etched into my brain. But theirs are not the only faces I see. All the *gifted* crap aside, I *was* a smart kid, and that meant I could hang around with *other* smart kids—a much nicer bunch.

I was never as smart as my friend Larry Penn. He was skinny and a natural athlete, with a big mop of hair. Through third grade we were neck-and-neck in school, but then he shot ahead like a rocket. For crying out loud, he was doing integral calculus in sixth grade.

If Dennis has a bike and rides it into a wind out of the north/northwest at nine miles per hour, and Phyllis buys two bushels of peaches for two dollars and fifty nine cents each, how much licorice can Blake afford if Zach stubs his toe.

I could barely follow the storyline, never mind trying to actually solve the problem.

Craig Basson was also smart. He was portly like me, with a blonde crewcut. He always had dried snot on his upper lip, and always had a cough. Back in first grade, he used to throw up at milk and cookies every day during naptime. Craig turned out to be a world-class cardiologist and heart surgeon, published in sixty-eight different medical journals, and Chief of Cardiac Medicine at New York Presbyterian Hospital, with privileges at seven other Manhattan hospitals. Not too shabby for a snot-nosed cougher with a weak gag reflex.

I was surrounded by really smart kids. The ironic part, is that however smart some of them were (and are) the entire *gifted* shtick of the Sands Point Academy was later exposed in a 1972 *New York Magazine* story as a strictly for-profit fraud. We weren't necessarily *gifted*—we just had parents with an obsession for excellence and enough money to back it up.

This was also a time in my life when I was suffering mightily from "asthma." I put it in quotes, I did not, in fact, have asthma. What I did have were parents who both smoked four packs of cigarettes a day. They'd even light up in the car with all the windows rolled up. *To keep the smoke IN?* I wasn't allowed to roll down my own window in the back. It wasn't asthma—it was acute secondhand smoke exposure—my little seven year-old lungs were inhaling roughly eight packs a day. Today, if someone lights up fifty feet away, my nose closes up and my eyes burn.

But to treat my "asthma," the ear, nose, and throat doctor we went to put me on a form of speed, which was the remedial drug for acute asthma. It was a drug called Marax, which was pretty much an early form of methamphetamine. The principal being, in order to get more oxygen to the lungs, let's jack up the heart like a trip hammer. So, quite often I was on speed while at school. Interesting how many of the "progress reports" from school often spoke about how *If Steven could just sit still, and not constantly speak out of turn, he would be a wonderful child to have in class.*

I was jacked up like a NASCAR pit crew on black beauties and they wanted me to sit still? Still, I skipped a grade, and was about eight years-old with the ten year-olds in fifth grade. One bright spot was that I'd begun to discover the joy of board games, and loved to play a game called Risk. One day during recess, I played a kid named Peter Carisi and kicked his ass all over the place. Peter, a wiry, bucktoothed ginger, had not yet mastered the art of losing gracefully, to a younger kid no less, and he threw the game pieces and board in the air. Risk had thousands of little pieces, and they landed everywhere. Then, before storming away, he fired a threat: "I will get you back."

I had no idea how devious his retribution would be.

The next day our teacher told us to get our coats and form a double line to be taken out for recess. I went and got my coat and I zipped myself up and waited patiently at the front of the line. All of a sudden, one after another, kids were crying, shouting and whining that they couldn't button up their coats because their buttons were gone. The teacher came over to investigate. Indeed, about two-thirds of the kids' coats had their buttons cut off. I stood and waited at the front of the line, not particularly interested in everyone else's troubles—after all, I had a zipper and my coat was fine.

But it was chaos.

The teacher basically staged an inquest to find the buttons and weed out the *psychopath* who would do such a thing. We were all deputized to search the classroom for the missing buttons—momentarily innocent before proven guilty—and we fanned out around the room like an impromptu search party.

Then one of the kids shouted, "Hey, look, I found them!"

He was standing in front of my cubbyhole. One cubby from the top, two up from the floor. *My cubby.* The buttons were there next to a pair of scissors to boot. I was framed. And I was sure it was Peter Carisi. Think about it. I supposedly cut off everyone's buttons, left them right at the edge of my cubby hole with the very scissors I used to commit the crime? The teacher took me in the hall and grilled me. "Why did you do this?! Why?!" All I could say, over and over again, was, "It wasn't me! I didn't do it!"

Peter Carisi must have been snickering across the hall. (He wasn't in the room because he was in a different section of the fifth grade.) I always knew it was him, but because of the code of *Omertà* I never gave him up. Are you kidding? I'm no rat! (Though I'm certainly ratting him out here. But the Statute of Limitations will probably keep him from having to serve retroactive detention.)

So I had no plausible alternative to suggest when the teacher asked, "Well, if you didn't do it, who did?" With a grip I remember like it was yesterday, her nails digging into my upper arm, she dragged me down the stairs, and across the lobby to the Headmaster's office.

The Headmaster, Dr. Benjamin Fine, was an old man that Sands Point Academy called a "world renowned child psychologist" in their marketing and advertising. He was later discredited in the *New York Magazine* piece as a senile old man with a padded resume. But there I was outside of his office. I guess I was going to meet with him, I wasn't sure. I sat for about an hour. Then my parents walked in, and were led past me to his office. Several minutes later, Fine invited me in too. There I was between my parents and this phony shrink—my mother was crying, and I don't remember the look on my dad's face—but Fine asked me, "Why did you cut your classmates' buttons off of their coats?" No presumption of innocence. No opportunity to explain myself. A rush to judgment. My only answer was, "I didn't do it." The doctor looked at my parents empathetically and said, "See, he lies. He's dangerous and angry and we need to get him help quickly."

I still don't really know how or why I went from being the kid who was so *gifted* he needed to skip a grade, to the kid who was *dangerous* and needed help. Maybe Peter's parents had pull. It just never occurred to anyone that I might be telling the truth. And *Omertà* aside, I wasn't smart enough to see that by keeping quiet, I was cutting off my nose to spite my face.

My parents took me home in their car.

They didn't believe me. The teacher didn't believe me. The headmaster didn't believe me. I begged them to, I did, even as I steadfastly refused to divulge my alternate theory of the crime. But they just couldn't believe me. My mother kept saying, "The one thing I can't stand is a liar."

Thankfully, I'm pretty sure my parents kept Poppy in the dark about it, so my new classification as an *angry, dangerous LIAR* didn't affect our close relationship. I wonder now why I didn't turn to him for help. Maybe I didn't want to let him down—I didn't want to change the way he thought about me.

A liar.

It wasn't just that I wasn't lying about that particular incident, I wasn't a child who lied very much at all. An occasional fib about who ate the cake or spilled cereal on the floor? Sure. Major lies? No.

But I made a decision that day.

I would never tell the truth or trust anyone ever again.

Why bother?

They sent me to a shrink named Dr. Gruber. His method of getting kids to open up was to play chess with them. I liked chess, but I was hip to his groove, and I had no intention of opening up—to him or to anyone. I was in therapy, for a crime I didn't commit. I did my best to not tell this man anything. I was diagnosed as hyperkinetic. That would later necessitate that I be put on Ritalin. Like the asthma meds I was already taking periodically, Ritalin is also a speed derivative and I don't believe any consideration was given at that time as to how those two medications would interact.

My progress reports, or as mine should have been called "regress" reports, always said the same thing. "He would be a wonderful student if he could just sit still." *Thanks Nostradamus.* I'm on two different kinds of speed. You connect yourself to a car battery with jumper cables on your temples and see if you sit still. These stimulants, along with the emotional tumult of being framed were causative factors, not excuses, for why I was becoming a problem child for real.

I started out as a boy who felt ashamed for no good reason.

Soon I would find plenty of valid reasons to be ashamed.

HE CALLED ME *PICKY*

After the Sands Point Academy there were a few harrowing years at a private school on Long Island called St. Paul's. It was an Episcopalian exclusive Caucasian boy's preparatory school. My inattentiveness, lousy attitude, and defensiveness over not being White enough was proving toxic to my scholastic career. I didn't fit in, but a silver lining appeared—my increasing size and sports ability brought some acceptance. I was a wrestler. The strange thing about wrestling, is that you need to be big enough to wrestle, but you constantly diet in order to stay in your weight class. In the end, I was not invited to continue my studies at St. Paul's because some diet pills I got from one of the other wrestlers to cut weight were discovered in my locker. The school just wouldn't stand for that, not to mention that my Mom already was coming to school on a weekly basis to meet with my teachers to discuss my behavior.

My shrink recommend we try boarding school.

My Dad had gone to a prestigious Christian prep school in Brooklyn called Poly Prep. So the idea of me going to a Christian prep school appealed to them—though not one as near as Brooklyn. They were looking for something farther away—*much* farther away—and I ended up in the summer program at South Kent School, in South Kent, Connecticut. The summer program was sort of an audition, to determine whether I would get in for the fall term.

Again, I had difficulty adjusting, but one man made all the difference, becoming the father that I never had before: George H. Barlett, my Latin teacher, and the school's headmaster, who immediately dubbed me "Picky," short for Pickman.

George was a gigantic man who stood roughly six foot four, and he was huge inside and out, and a true man of faith, who lived by spiritual values of single mindedness of purpose, kindness, compassion for all people, and, most of all, love. Especially for his students. He knew how to love all of us differently, each how we needed it. We all need love, but George was one part orchestra conductor, one part spiritualist, and all human. He was not only my Latin teacher, but my life coach before anyone had made up the term.

I was good at Latin. In that summer program I made two friends, one of whom I'm still close with today, Richard Gregory, and the other, my arch rival because of his Philadelphia sports fanaticism, Jim Hickox. I was an Islanders fan, he rooted for the Flyers. I was a Mets fan, he the Phillies. I was a Giants fan, Jim loved the Eagles. We were set opposite each other in a way I'd never experienced, and it created a friendship that gave me the one kid I could argue with and occasionally triumph over since these were the years that my Islanders won four consecutive Stanley Cups—the first one coming in overtime on Long Island against his beloved Flyers. Many fall and winter afternoons were filled with Jim and me warring over which team or player was better and how the other one sucked.

I got into South Kent that fall—just barely, I later learned at a reunion event. South Kent was a paradisiacal place on a hillside in the Berkshires of New England, nestled above ponds and lakes. The faculty was determined to teach young people how to work together as a team, but most importantly, how to WORK. We mopped, mowed and did our own dishes. Every student was assigned to a work area headed up by an upperclassman. Yes there were kitchen staff and maintenance men for the much bigger job of lodging and feeding four hundred people every day, but the spit and polish, the pride, and the elbow grease was left to the kids. Seniors ran the school, meted out discipline and basically ran herd over the underclassmen. Like the Sands Point bus rides, I was often the butt of the joke. I was five feet tall and rotund. The seniors called me Fat Pickman, Kool Aid, and once again, Fat Albert. But I started firing back with humor, and with a precision that I make a living from today. I didn't know to be grateful then, but now I thank God for the experience.

All-boys Episcopalian prep school in Connecticut.

Attendance at daily church services was mandatory, and regardless of your religious background or inclinations, we were in chapel seven days a week. I was raised a Jew, so that seemed like a lot, but even for the *Goyim* it seemed a bit excessive.

At SKS, if you were White, it was all good.

If you were Jewish, you'd get some shit.

If you were Black there would be some ugly slurs.

If you were Jewish AND Black, well, you can just imagine.

Looking back, I'm grateful for my ethnicity because it not only made me very, very different from the other boys, but demanded that I be in a constant state of preparedness for whatever insults or attitudes I had to endure.

The grades were called forms. Ninth grade/third form, tenth/fourth form and so on, modeled after the British form school system. Sixth formers were seniors, revered by faculty and students alike, whose privileges were coveted by underclassmen. Heading up the sixth form were prefects who were elected to head not just the senior class, but the whole school. Another intended benefit of a school like this was that you went to school and lived with your professors and their families and they got to know you very well— better than you would have liked in some cases. They were our coaches, our mentors, and friends in some cases, as each master (as they were termed) had differing styles—with varying degrees of formality. Of course, they had favorites, and I learned at my twenty-fifth reunion that I was actually the favorite of more than a few of our masters, for my intelligence, wit and *colorful* personality. Who knew?

George Bartlett and his cool, artistic wife, Maggie, had a way of making every child feel like he was theirs. The Bartletts were sort of the First Family of South Kent when I was there, and if it were not for them, I'm not sure I would have made it through the White, Christian gauntlet of South Kent intact. My relationship with George and Maggie gave me a cachet—and kept teasing and bullying from going too far. I was a frequent visitor to their on-campus home, allowed to eat "special foods" to attempt to stay on a diet. They had four kids: Polly, who graduated before I attended, Peter, two years older than I, Benjamin, two years younger, and my classmate Liney, who was my age. I was at the Bartlett house so much, it was like I became their fifth kid. I think their children were aware of the special relationship I was afforded with their Dad, and I'd like to thank them from the bottom of my heart for sharing him with me. If not for George's presence in my life at that moment in my development, I promise you I would not have made it through puberty.

George also administered my Ritalin, and many mornings when he would dole them out to me, we'd spend an hour in his office, the hub of the "Old Building," just shooting the shit. These sessions were like therapy for me. Surrounded by often cruel, sometime racist, kids, our chats kept me from going over the edge. This is when I was in the depths of living in a state of constant shame. Even though I was fourteen, I had yet to understand the brutal jokes aimed at anyone of a different race or religion, so, once again, I personalized the hatred.

I thought people hated me, and quite frankly, that made ME hate me. On the outside, my strong personality and sense of humor prevailed, but inside, I was dying. It wasn't until George Bartlett retired years later, and invited me back to the ceremony in his honor, that I would fully realize the depth of his love for me. Out of all the thousands of students that he would mentor, George requested that I be the man to give him a sendoff speech. What an honor. His presence in my life not only saved me then, but bolstered me twenty-five years later in a way that made ME feel like the honoree at HIS testimonial. Sheer parental genius on George's part, because even a quarter of a century out of the nest, the honor of being THE student chosen to speak about him in front of colleagues and hundreds of students felt like vindication for all the frightening and emotionally uncertain years of my life. The debt I owe him for being the exact kind of father figure I needed at that time in my life can never be repaid—but I can honor it by how I live my life today and always. In the same way that I was Poppy's gift to his daughter, George H. Bartlett was the universe's gift to me. Many times when I was overly loud, which was often, or was out of bounds, George would look at me and say "Picky, Picky, Picky" and it would reel me back in.

But there was also a tragic irony.

At the precise moment that my relationship with George was developing, my Poppy was becoming more and more diminished by Alzheimer's disease. At the time, Alzheimer's was not yet a diagnosis, and no one could say for sure what Poppy was going through, but his immense, vibrant persona was now gone. All day, he sat in his chair staring blankly at the television. He was at home, the way my Nanny wanted it, with round-the-clock nurses to tend to his bodily functions and his moment-to-moment care. A once proud, talkative man who loved to joke and banter, he was reduced to a lump of virtually lifeless humanity. Down the stretch, he would never speak or react to anything with one exception. When I would visit, I'd sit very close to him on his left in the den. I would tell him jokes in his ear and at the punchline, he would laugh uncontrollably. The laughter made him drool, and Nanny would rush over with a handkerchief to wipe his chin, every time announcing, "He's not supposed to laugh." What utter stupidity. I was excited that he reacted to anything at all when we visited. So soon, I'd be at it again, and the whole process would be repeated. *He's not supposed to laugh...*

The disease took him later that same year. I remember vividly getting called down to the Old Building to Mr. B's office. He broke the bad news to me and told me that I'd be taken to the train to make the one hundred twenty-mile trip home for the funeral. I was in shock, I wept, and I was crushed.

Although my Dad's father had died when I was about seven, I was too young to understand it. Poppy's death was different. I felt the full brunt of the pain and loss, and it was months before I'd get my smile back. But sure enough, George was there to catch me in the most difficult time of my life.

But making my Poppy laugh is what I remember of our last visits, and I know he would have been so proud of what I've become. Every night before I go on stage to perform, while on my knees in whatever dressing room I'm in, I dedicate my performance to my Poppy. I picture him in the front row, laughing and enjoying my show. In my heart, he's part of everything I do, because I was his gift to my family, and he was my biggest fan, from the day before I was born, until the day he left in December, 1977.

I had other duties at South Kent beyond cleaning and scrubbing, and doing my schoolwork. I was also the church organist. It was tradition that the role be filled by a student, and with my ability to play by ear, I guess I was a natural choice. Two minor confessions: During long evening prayer services when the sacrament was administered, I might have snuck back into the sacristy during the gospel and sampled the wafer hosts and the wine—on more than one occasion. Also, I did not enjoy my "organ lessons" with the music master when his hand was rubbing my leg.

Playing the organ in church might be one of the toughest things I've ever accomplished. I had to learn roughly four hundred hymns by ear through trial and error because I certainly didn't know what was printed on the sheet music. The other thing, and this is daunting, the sound from the pipes when you hit the keys and foot pedals comes from all the way in the back of the chapel in the organ pipe loft. Meaning, there's a significant delay of about two seconds, so confidence is key given that you hit the keys and the sound is not immediate. For all of fourth form year, I struggled through the hymns, and on many nights, no one had any idea what I was playing during the singing of the hymn, least of all me. I faked my way through three years of *organ grinding*. It's their fault for making a Jew play their Christian hymns.

I played Varsity Football, Hockey and Crew. That's right, I said Crew. You want to lose your mind, row on a crew team. OMG. Cardiovascular fire breathing. Crew's definitely a slavery sport. You must keep up with the other seven guys in your shell or you screw up the whole synchronization of the boat. You're stuck in a boat in the middle of a lake with Mini-Me with a megaphone, screaming at you, "ROW, ROW, ROW fat Black Jew, ROW!" Singularly one of the most demanding physical things I've ever attempted or accomplished. CREW. Never again.

At this point in my life, I still hadn't had sex yet, even though many of my classmates were already well versed in the ways of the flesh. I was also a virgin to alcohol and drugs, though my compadres were veterans—smoking in the woods, and getting blasted on the beer and weed circuit. When I finally did start to explore, there was one dalliance that illustrates just how cool George Bartlett could be.

We had a dance at a school called Ethel Walker which was about ninety minutes away. We periodically had these dances with an all-girls school just to *get the poison out*—at the time I had no idea what that meant. Dances were the most terrifying experience I could imagine. First of all, I felt that I was a horrible dancer. The part of me that should have been black was Jewish, and in that context, that's not the only part of me that could be explained that way. I had ZERO experience with the ladies. Not at home on Long Island, where I was an outcast because I didn't go to school with the local kids, or in school where it was all boys except for teachers' kids and the nurse. I was not smooth at these shindigs and my goal was to avoid female contact at all cost. The catastrophic anxiety attack would begin as our bus rolled onto the girls' school property and usually didn't abate until we returned to our campus and I was out of earshot of everyone else's conquest stories. At the dance I stayed by the snacks and ate cheese puffs with whatever teacher was the chaperone for the event. However, at the Ethel Walker dance, fifth form year, eleventh grade, I spread my wings and soared. *I actually ventured to the other side of the gym where the dance was held!* I saw a girl that was gorgeous to me and her name turned out to be Madeline. Her father was a bigwig in Florida, the governor or a senator or something. I don't remember anything but ending up under the raised paddle tennis courts on campus. I remember kissing for what seemed like hours and having a very painful bulge in my slacks, which I later learned was *blue balls*. After we emerged from beneath the courts, my watch said ten after ten. The bus back to school leaves at ten sharp, and if you're not on it, you were expelled from school.

My fate was sealed.

After my very first make-out session, I was going to get thrown out of school. Madeline ran in one direction without even saying goodbye, and I could see that the bus was gone. I walked out to the stone gate of the school and the only light for miles was the one illuminating the Ether Walker School for Girls sign. I was terrified to call school, because I knew I was out, so I sat and sat and sat for hours. Finally, I mustered up the courage to walk along the road and look for a gas station and after walking for what must have been forty-five minutes, I spotted a phone booth. I called the school's main number collect and guess who answers the phone and accepts the charges: George Bartlett. Wonderful. Before I could get one word out, he said "Picky is that you?" I squeezed out a "Yes." He said, "Stay where you are and I'll be there in an hour and a half." I had plenty of time to think about my fate, and I just knew I was packing tonight and being taken to the train tomorrow morning.

After what seemed like hours, I saw headlights coming from down the road. It was Mr. B. in the school pickup truck. He pulled around and told me to get in. We drove silently for about twenty minutes which felt like an eternity. I was looking straight ahead at the light from the headlamps on the road frozen. George broke the silence with "So Picky, did you get some?" I wasn't sure what he was asking so I said "Get some what?" He fired back through chuckle "Nookie, Picky, did you get some nookie?" I hesitated for what must have been a minute and again wasn't sure what he meant, so I replied "Kinda, yeah kinda." "Kinda?" he said, "I'm driving three extra hours tonight for you to KINDA get some nookie?!" I really had no idea what he was talking about, so embarrassed beyond belief, I asked, "What's nookie?" He laughed and said "Mouth to mouth, fun stuff, TLC. Did you have some fun with any girls?" "Oh, yes, yes, nookie, I got nookie sir, I'm all nookied out." He laughed and said "Good." We drove the rest of the way in total silence and he drove me up the hill to my dormitory. As I got out of the truck he said "Good night Picky, let this evening be between us." I breathed for the first time in four hours. We were going to keep it between us. He knew I was a rookie. He knew this was probably my first time with a girl EVER. He was cool. I wasn't expelled. I was understood. I was loved.

When you go to a prep school the likes of South Kent, it's assumed you'll go on to college, hence, the *prep* in prep school. Becoming a prep COOK seemed more of a likely career path for me, but after acquitting myself well on my SAT exams, I decided that I wanted to go to Emory University in Atlanta. My grades were not up to snuff, but my board scores were nothing to sneeze at. Emory, fancying itself the *Harvard of the South* was not exactly anxious to secure my attendance. But I have an indomitable spirit, and I wrote a letter and mailed it to the director of admissions EVERY SINGLE DAY until he cried uncle and sent me an acceptance letter.

My Dad and I went for a campus visit in Atlanta, and best I can remember it might have been the only good time we'd ever had together, just my father and me. We are intrinsically very different people. I'm an extrovert, he an introvert. I'm very liberal, and he's very conservative. I'm very tolerant and accepting of people's differences, he is not. I love, love, LOVE sports. He detests them. So there's very little common ground. Our only real bond is that we both love my Mom. We aren't even flesh and blood. And there it is, the underbelly of my feelings toward my adoption. *Dad and I are nothing alike because we aren't one another's flesh and blood.* Nature over nurture? I don't know, but it matters. The Atlanta trip was filled with optimism, however, and we were easy and even-tempered with each other. It was a highlight, and I'm grateful we got to share the experience.

Graduation day at South Kent School is called "Prize Day" and I received the Music Prize for excellence. The speaker was Vietnam War hero Admiral James B. Stockdale, who ultimately ran for vice president as Ross Perot's running mate. His boys Sid, Stan and Taylor all attended SKS and were legacy boys. As best as I can remember, Admiral Stockdale gave a great speech. Maybe he should have saved it for the debates in 1992, because the speech he gave that night became a *Saturday Night Live* satire legend.

I know I wouldn't have graduated without George's love and support, and I'm truly thankful. He was the unconditionally loving father presence that I had only felt from my Poppy, who had died earlier that year. The void in my life was filled—if temporarily—and I wouldn't find this kind of love again until my addiction had taken me all the way down to where it would take me. As I look back on my life I see several other men in my life at key times who saved me when I was on the brink of total personal disaster, but none the likes of the great George H. Bartlett. Thank you South Kent. Thank you George. I will always love you both.

TWO COLLEGES... WASTED

From the Moment my Dad and I visited Emory University, I knew I wanted to be in Atlanta. I'd be lying if I said that it was the beautiful campus, or Atlanta itself, or that I had an intense desire to make my prep school education pay off.

I was there because the girls were gorgeous.

I had never been around girls, save my make-out session at the girls' school under the paddle tennis courts. I was blown away by the Emory girls—their hair, their accents, the way they dressed.

That's what propelled me to write all those letters to the admissions director, each day outlining how much of an asset I'd be to the Emory community. I stressed my work ethic, my humble roots at a work/study prep school in Connecticut. My record three-year streak of attending Episcopalian services while maintaining my connection to the Jewish community and simultaneously observing Black History month. I don't know how many letters I sent. Ten? Twenty? A hundred? But I got the magic envelope, with the admissions director's invitation to join the Emory University community. I was ecstatic. I'd done what no one thought was possible. I turned an underachiever's prep school transcript into an acceptance at one of the most respected college's in the country.

The school was a quarter system school, meaning, their calendar ran on quarters instead of semesters. In short, that meant that there was a final exam every four days. This school was so academic that there were no intercollegiate athletics and we had Wednesdays off so kids could catch up from the avalanche of work they had to do from Monday and Tuesday. Pressure? Not at Emory (wink, wink, nudge, nudge). Every student's parents were encouraged to purchase a stall at the library for their little genius, so they'd be able to spend the rumored thirty hours a week they needed to complete the mountain of assigned work. Everyone was pre-something: Pre-Med, Pre-Law. I was pre-nervous breakdown. I had no idea what I wanted to become, I was just glad to be somewhere where the ladies roamed free. When I arrived there, Emory was neck-and-neck with Cornell for most suicides on campus. It was so bad that one of the fraternities on campus painted a target logo on the plaza below the eight-story library. Kids were actually jumping to their death from the library. Pressure for sure, but the only pressure I took seriously, was the pressure to lose my virginity.

The first few weeks of school the fraternities and sororities were hosting parties to take their pick of the new meat on campus. We'd basically roam from frat party to frat party hoping that someone from one of them would invite us back to hang with the guys. There was the "jock" frat, "the Jewy frat," "the KKK frat," the "Pre-Med frat," the "preppy frat." There was even a frat for the losers. If you weren't invited to join anywhere, you pretended you didn't care and declared yourself independent—*Indy*. I went to all of them and mixed and mingled. There were two with guys that dressed and sounded like the guys I spent the last seven years with in prep school. I felt most comfortable at Sigma Chi. I figured I was a shoe-in because I'd been dressing like these guys and hanging with guys like them since I was ten years-old. WRONG. They saw me as Black, and well, you know the rest. So, I, like all the other *unselecteds*, I decided to pretend I didn't give a fuck.

There was an ice hockey club on campus and I joined. We played an intercollegiate schedule but didn't have funding from the university. We were the Emory Ice Eagles and we sucked. Our coach was a chain-smoking, drunk, seventy-five year-old guy named "Crusty" Bill Young. I don't even know how he came to be the coach, but he was. We practiced an hour and a half from campus, at the only ice rink available. It was where the Atlanta Flames practiced, though, so the only ice time we could get was at night. I made some great friends almost immediately, Keith Schwartz from Plainview, Long Island being one. He was a junior, and an *Indy*, and he made being an outcast from the fraternity system seem cool. My other pal was maybe the slowest, lousiest goalie on ice anywhere, but the sweetest, best human being ever. Mitch "Red Light" Rosenberg. Who ever heard of a Jewish hockey goalie, but he was ours. Alright, he had a good glove hand, but his stick side was like the Texas-Mexican border, porous and wide open. He's a lifelong friend of mine to this day, but Mitch couldn't stop a shot if the puck were a basketball. I played defense in front of him, but when Mitch was in goal, you had better block the shot, 'cause if it whizzed past YOU, it was definitely going past Mitch.

We lost almost ALL of our games but we had fun. We even had a female on the team. Liz Corson, from Maine. Everybody made fun of her but she had balls to be out there playing hockey with the guys. As a matter of fact, as I'm about to share, she was probably out there BECAUSE of the guys.

Halloween, 1979.

I was eighteen, and the closest I'd ever gotten to getting laid was still my one time with Madeline under the paddle tennis courts at Ethel Walker in Simsbury, Connecticut.

One night during hockey practice, I had to go to the bathroom—number two—which, with hockey pants and garters and skates was a whole production. It would have been easier to shoot myself in the leg and wait for the paramedics to cut the whole getup off me. I waddled off the ice to the men's room, found an empty stall, sat down, and started making the requisite guy noises that come with celebrating a great bowel movement. Part congratulating yourself for making it there, part cries of ecstasy and relief. I looked to my left and saw another pair of skates in the stall next door. I was instantly embarrassed but not so much, until I heard a young ladies voice said "Sounds wonderful." It was Liz. OMG. I was mortified. She inquired "What are you doing for Halloween?" I said "Nothing, why?" She said "I'm having a costume party and I very much would like for you to come." *Finally a party to which I AM invited. Perfect. I'm there.* Liz was a solid seven, with curly dark hair and blue eyes. Okay, she was definitely on the masculine side—she drove a pickup truck, played hockey with the guys, and used the men's room—but she was still beautiful.

As Halloween approached I decided on a costume: *I'm in Atlanta. How's about the quarterback of the Falcons, Steve Bartkowski?* I went to a sporting goods store and bought the entire uniform from helmet to cleats, eye-black and all. Weird choice as I look back, but it didn't matter, since my life would change on that night. I showed up at Liz's apartment exactly on time. I knocked on the door. She was dressed as a witch, holding a cup of beer, and she invited me into her apartment. There were no decorations. Just a keg of Stroh's beer and some candy corn in a dish on the coffee table. She pumped me a beer from the keg and told me to make myself comfortable.

I sat on the couch. She handed me the beer and sat down right next to me, very close. "Who else is coming?" I asked. "Oh, I don't know," she replied, "We're here."

Yes we are.

Then she picked up a lighter and a Pepsi can with aluminum foil on top, lit something, and sucked the side of the can. It was a converted beverage can/pot pipe. I'd never seen this before but, okay, I was thinking—*I know her, she's my teammate, there's nothing to be afraid of.* I tried to smoke the Pepsi can, but I didn't even know where to put the flame.

Then she showed me how to take a hit.

I wish I'd never taken that first hit, because the eleven years that followed were punctuated with thousands and thousands of hits of anything and everything that could be smoked to make you high. That first one was the push out of the plane they give you when you skydive. I fell for over a decade. Truth be told, I wouldn't change a thing because who am I to argue with destiny or divine order, but every once in a while you wonder.

I remember scaling the stairs to her bedroom.

I remember her on top of me.

I remember I wasn't wearing my pants.

I remember I WAS wearing my jersey, shoulder pads, and cleats.

Liz had me inside of her, and she was riding me like one of those bulls at country ranch bars. Her hair was going faster than her head and so were her breasts. Then she collapsed on the bed next to me and I was blocked in on the inside of the bed next to the window.

I laid awake all night while she snored and tumbled and put her arm around my chest. I was waiting for my moment to get the hell out of there, but there just never seemed to be an opportunity. I felt like jumping out the window without my pants, but I could have broken one or both of my legs, and we had a hockey game against Alabama next week. So I waited, and I waited. Thank GOD she rolled over. *Here's my chance to climb over her, find my padded football pants, and scram.* I successfully climbed over Liz sleeping on her side. I stepped off the bed, tip-toeing in my cleats to the door. I was right there, hand on doorknob, when I heard Liz say "You're staying for breakfast aren't you?" Stuttering and fumferring, all I could get out was, "I have a term paper I need to finish."

I found the keys to my royal blue Cutlass 442 and bounded out the door. Once I got to the car, I realized I'd forgotten my helmet, but I didn't care, I was finally out of there. I had lost my virginity and it was nothing like what I had imagined. It was worse. I was dominated and manhandled, and as best as I could figure out, no love was involved. So that was that. I lost my virginity to beer, marijuana, and lust.

There'd be many, many more beers.

There'd be acres of weed smoked in the years to come.

But the sex was a little harder to come by after that night.

Like a moron, I went directly to Keith's house to tell him what happened. I had no idea that this would open the flood gates of jokes and insults about losing my virginity to Liz.

Keith had great pot also.

Seems like everyone did. I noticed that when I smoked it, I didn't feel the overwhelming sense of fear and anxiety in social situations that were my constant companions. I tensed up around the opposite sex without booze and pot. With it, I was free and funny—*chatty*—and unafraid of women. Unafraid of *anything*.

One day, I was hanging in the student union in the Coke Lounge, where they had a piano. (Emory was a primary beneficiary of Coca-Cola Company largesse. As a matter of fact, Robert W. Woodruff donated one hundred million dollars in Coke stock to the university. That was thirty-five years ago. Emory is now one of the most phenomenally appointed college campuses in the country.) Anyway, there was a piano there and I hadn't played since the last church service at South Kent School months ago. I sat down and while I'm ashamed to admit I like Barry Manilow music, then, I absolutely worshipped him. Billy Joel and Barry Manilow were the soundtrack of my childhood and teen years. So, I'm playing some Manilow and a girl comes in and comes over to the piano and leans over it watching me while I played. Play "Weekend in New England." I was like, "That's easy." She was *kvelling*. I was showing off. Then she sat down and played, and she was damn good too. We bonded over that piano and I was obsessed with her. *Andrea*. Her name was *Andrea*. And I loved Andrea. She was striking, with dark hair and an animated, angular face—but it was the music that drew us together in the beginning. I had one other friend at Emory, Mike Crowley from Scarsdale, New York. We called him White Chocolate because he played basketball as well as the Black players. He was this Irish-Catholic guy, round, actually kind of rotund, with reddish brown hair and rosy cheeks. We were outcasts together from the frat system, and we ate, drank, and chased girls together. Once I met Andrea, though, I spent every spare moment with her. I hoped with all my heart that it would go better with her than it did my first time out, assuming that we would have sex. I did everything I could think of to get into her pants, but I never did. We were inseparable… but NO SEX. She was the daughter of two shrinks from Ramsey, New Jersey, inexperienced, and afraid. I *understood*, but I didn't *understand*. I was hurt. Very hurt.

I stopped going to class and just got stoned all the time.

This was a school where you could be a 4.0 student and fall behind easily. I didn't really care. At the end of freshman year I received a note from the dean of students informing me that my GPA was .9—POINT NINE—like on a scale of A-F, my GPA was an E. *But they didn't throw me out.* Amazing. The dean did warn me, though, that unless I pulled my GPA up a full point to a 1.9 in the first quarter of the following year, they would have no choice but to academically exclude me from the Emory community. In other words: *Throw me out.*

I came back the next fall for my second year, determined not to be academically excluded. I attended every class, took every quiz, studied, I even went to the library. I was still getting wasted all the time, but I applied myself like never before. I don't even remember my course load but here's the skinny: *I almost did it.* Against all odds, I got four As and an A-minus, bringing me one hundredth of a point to the necessary 1.9. I was stuck at 1.89, and the dean's office made it clear that there was no wiggle room—not even a measly hundredth of a point. The A-minus was the problem. It was my Political Science professor, who gave me an A on my term paper, I got an A on the mid-term, and an A on the final. But he marked me down for poor attendance, and in the grading, attendance weighed one-third of your grade with the tests and paper. He would not budge. I told him that I'd never miss a class again, I'd wax his car, re-roof his house. He wasn't budging. And that was that. I was out. I received a note from the dean of students which basically said, "Too little too late." Bye-bye freckle boy. *So close.* I was capable of doing the work, but incapable of actually following the rules. *Not fair!* Right? But I was the one who didn't follow the rules, and Emory stuck to their guns. Now? I think it was basically my fault. Then? It was totally NOT my fault—it was ANYONE'S fault but mine.

Talk about ashamed. I didn't want anyone to find out about it—eighteen months in, I had failed out of college.

Academically excluded my ass. I *failed*.

I came up with a Plan-B. I called Boston University, where I'd also been accepted as a senior at prep school. They wanted to know what I'd been doing since high school. I erased my failure at Emory by saying I'd been working for the family business—but wanted to start at Boston University next term. No problem.

I told my parents I was transferring to Boston University from Emory, when in fact, I would be starting over as a brand new freshman. It was dishonest and cowardly—but I'm also struck by how inventive and proactive it was to find a solution to the problem that would satisfy everyone involved.

If only I could have been that ingenious about my actual studies.

My Dad flew down and drove home with me in the Cutlass, which incidentally had so little braking power, we had to down shift to slow the car down to make exits. We drove from Atlanta to New York in eighteen hours, no stops, and ironically, no stopping ability.

How we made that drive with no brakes I'll never know. I don't know *why* either. Why was it so important to make the trip without stopping? Could my father and I really not bear to spend any more time than that together?

I entered Boston University in the winter of 1981, telling no one in my family that I was a freshman again, though I should have been a mid-year sophomore. I was too ashamed to admit that I had failed out at Emory. I lived in the freshman dorm on the thirteenth floor in the C-Tower of a legendary building called Warren Towers, or more affectionately the Zoo. Aptly named. It *was* a zoo, of three thousand freshmen—a cinder block high-rise of hormones and pot smoke.

There was a nucleus of guys who earlier that year dubbed

themselves the "Rude Boys." Just by living there, I was one of them. There was a tall, skinny, brown-haired stoner guy named Jim Terwilliger on the other side of the hall, and within a few minutes of talking to Jim he was calling me "Sarge." I was like "My name is Steve" he was like "Okay Saaaaaaaarge." I had a nickname! They all called me Sarge, and I had never really been popular or accepted anywhere like that before, so I loved the approval. Sarge it was, Sarge I became, and Sarge I still am.

I hated the mandated freshman courses in the Liberal Arts College of the University. There were so many other courses I DID want to take. So I gamed the system. This was pre-computers, so exploiting loopholes was a lot easier. There was a protocol if you wanted to drop out of one class and add another. All you had to do was attend the class you wanted to be in, get the professor to sign your triplicate drop/add form, and submit it to the registrar's office.

I was a fully paid matriculated student so I simply attended four classes I DID want to take, and signed out of the four mandatory ones I DIDN'T want to take. Presto! I had my very own customized course load. Then came the loophole jackpot: About a month into attending classes, I got a call from the bursar's office: "We have a check here for you. Would you like us to send it home, to your campus mailbox, or would you like to come pick it up here at 881 Commonwealth Avenue?" I told her, "I'll be right over."

I jumped on the T, Boston's above ground transit, which was free anywhere on the B.U. campus. I bounded off and headed into the administration building, took the elevator upstairs, and followed the signs to the bursar's office. I didn't know what a bursar was, but they had a check for me, and I'd never gotten a check from anyone before, so I was happy to show up. I waited on line, up to a window where a woman coldly said, "Student I.D. please." I handed it under the bulletproof bank window slot. She went through some envelopes and said "Ah, here it is, Mr. Pickman." She slid the envelope under the window. I grabbed it and bolted for the elevator, afraid she'd call me back and say that there was a mistake. I got on the elevator and fingered open the envelope.

THE CHECK WAS FOR FIVE THOUSAND FOUR HUNDRED AND FIFTY DOLLARS!

Practically holding my breath the whole way, I took the T to Kenmore Square directly to Bank of Boston and opened a bank account. *Why? Who? What happened?* I was rich, and could afford just about anything, so I wasn't asking any questions. I certainly didn't call home and mention my newfound wealth.

Each semester I'd repeat this drop/add class scenario, and each semester I'd be called to pick up a huge check. I later learned that the loophole within the loophole in the system, was that if you dropped out of classes you had already paid for at the start of the semester— *or if your parents had already paid for them*—they'd refund you for those, and still add you to the new classes WITHOUT CHARGING YOU. It wasn't just a loophole, it was a miracle.

Extra money. Classes I liked. The weed was plentiful. And trips to Connecticut to get illegal grain alcohol were frequent. Garbage pails of Hawaiian Punch and grain and weed. We had the party room. My roommate was a talented guy named John Hyatt Choate, and he was face down on the bed from a night of heavy vodka consumption the first day I walked into the dorm room, and seldom missed a night of partying in the three years we roomed together. Hyatt was from New Canaan, Connecticut White aristocracy. He was a tall, dark-haired James Dean-handsome dude, who lived for alternative rock, and played the drums really, really well. Every woman he met wanted him. They befriended me hoping to get to him—I was like his social bodyguard. He was as close to a best friend as I ever had in my life. We were pals from two different worlds, but we loved each other as friends and hung as roommates in two different dorms, until our lives took different turns and we fell out of touch. (Later, he went on to produce the famous Michael Jackson commercial for Pepsi, the one where Jackson's hair caught on fire.)

I smoked pot every single day.

It didn't hurt that there was a dealer living on my hallway, buddy from Jersey named Jim Dorf who had the only computer in the building—RIGHT IN HIS ROOM! Computers are as necessary as food and water for every college student today. But then, a computer was so exotic, so *dangerous*, that it was actually considered contraband. If you were discovered with a computer in your room, you faced expulsion from the dorm. Maybe they were right. Jim kept track of all his pot sales on that computer—he was a mad programmer and hacker who actually built the computer himself. He wore round glasses and was always smiling—since he was always stoned. He gave me free ounces if I helped him weigh and bag the weed. We'd do bong hits and listen to Pink Floyd on his turntable. A turntable is a device that plays vinyl records by spinning them around while a needle scratches the surface and plays the music from grooves in the record. Sounds funny doesn't it. Today we walk around with seventy-one million songs in our phones. In those days you had a milk crate you stole from behind a supermarket that held a hundred records.

I fell into the same pattern of smoking weed, drinking, sleeping in, and not going to class. I went through two and a half aimless years this way until I found the B.U. School of Public Communications. They had advertising and public relations, and film and television classes. *I want to do this. This I can do.* Midway through what should have been my junior year I got into the School of Public Communications. S.P.C. was right up my alley—project oriented courses, NO TEXT BOOKS and literally NO TESTS. My kind of college.

I was finally going to class and soaking it up because all of the classes offered in this section of the university were project oriented and the professors were cool. Two in particular were Walter Lubars and Bob Montgomery. They were ad-men back when ad-men were

AD-MEN. Sort of like *Mad Men*, but not as much booze. Walter was an award-winning copywriter and creative director, and Bob, the chief of his own agency. They created a student run advertising agency at B.U. called Ad Lab. Students would occupy the different jobs in the advertising agency creative process and service actual accounts in Boston, mostly charities like the Red Cross, the New England Home for Little Wanderers (an orphanage), and many others. It was in this program that I had finally found my legs. I loved it. It tapped into my creative mind and working on REAL creative materials for REAL accounts gave me a place to shine. We created ad campaigns, brochures and even in a few instances shot public service announcement television spots.

One day, while having an Ad Lab meeting in the theater-sized class room, I went on stage and from the podium pitched my *colleagues* an idea to have an advertising awards dinner, in effect enabling us to celebrate ourselves for the amazing job we were doing creating advertising. "We'll invite industry pros to come in and judge our work and we'll name the awards after our amazing mentors, Walter Lubars and Bob Montgomery. We'll call them the "Lu-Mont" awards." My plans went on and on, including getting a ballroom at a prestigious downtown hotel, and throwing a world class shin-dig just like the world famous CLIO Awards. I don't know where or why I got the idea, but people began adding more ideas and before you know it, we were voting to do the "Lu-Monts."

Assessing this turn of events, Walter Lubars got up, took a long draw on his meerschaum Sherlock Holmes-style pipe. "Thank you," he said, "This is all very flattering, but how are WE gonna pay for it?" I quickly interrupted. "We'll do a fundraiser! And we'll raise all the money we need to have the dinner." Bob Montgomery piped in, "Dinner? Now it's a dinner? I thought it was an awards night." I said, "We'll raise enough money to eat too." I had never run an awards night, let alone a dinner, oh, and you can throw fundraiser in too, but

I opened my mouth in front of a hundred and fifty students, so I had no choice. I was going to do this. *We.* I mean *We* were going to do it.

By then I lived in a dorm called Myles Standish Hall, right behind the CITGO sign in Kenmore Square. It was a converted old hotel with spacious rooms that all had floor-to-ceiling windows that opened so you could sit on the window sill and even see the world famous "Green Monstaahhhh of Fenway Pahhhhk."

I'd just done a couple of bong hits of some "primo" sensimillia when I got THE IDEA for the fundraiser. *We'll do a fashion show!* We can start with a model search from all over campus. Why not? B.U. has thirty-six thousand students! We could do a casting cattle call, publicize it in the student newspaper, the *Freep*, (Short for *The Free Press*) and use students from every school in the university. Management, Fine Arts, Medical, Liberal Arts, Engineering, Computer Science, Law, etc. The on-campus event of the year! Who wouldn't come and heckle their friends *modeling*?

Everyone in Ad Lab loved the idea, and after wading through piles and piles of big university red tape, we got the Big Room at the student union. All the members of Ad Lab worked in the various areas of expertise that we needed, hence making this into a gigantic self-created project, all devised, conceived and executed BY ME thank you. Public relations kids did the public relations. Art directors designed posters, brochures, and newspaper ads for the *Freep*. Account executives solicited retail stores on Boston's fashionable Newbury Street for clothes and accessories. We got a pet store to supply dogs and exotic birds in some of the scenes. Dozens of stores signed on. We got TONS of stuff from Neiman-Marcus, because David Marcus, made one phone call and hooked us right up with the Copley Square store.

But one more thing.... Hmmmmm... Who would be the master of ceremonies of this cavalcade of amateurs masquerading as fashionistas? ME of course. Roll in the piano, I'll EMCEE and play the piano. We'll videotape it, and have photography students running around like paparazzi flashing shots of the action. A red carpet? You betcha!

In retrospect, I was really putting this whole thing together so I would have an event to host. I wanted to host it, and I had no competition for the job. I don't know why it became so important to me, but I was going to be the *Emcee to End All Emcees*. I'd never emceed anything before, but I was burning to, *itching* to, so I did.

The big night came.

The models were fabulous.

The clothes were fabulous.

We sold every last ticket and raised something like seven thousand dollars, which would be around eleven million dollars today.

And everyone said the emcee was fabulous. *Really they did!* I deftly made fun of every outfit that came down the runway and the audience of my peers roared with laughter. Then I played Billy Joel on the piano. Then some impromptu, stream-of-consciousness one-liners. It was a major rush. I didn't know it then, but, I was well and truly bitten by the bug. I loved making people laugh. Yeah, I'd gotten laughs before from old men at the card tables, and small groups of friends, but this was different. This was a huge crowd, and it was… *intoxicating*. I didn't know yet that THIS was an intoxication that could be way better than the other kind.

The fashion show was a major triumph for me.

I had no idea that it would mark the end of my stint at Boston University.

BOSTON FASHION

The Monday after the fashion show, I was at the Ad Lab office with Grant Sanders, a talented art director, still stoned from the morning *wake and bake*. Wet index-fingering my way through the *Boston Herald* to see if there's any mention of our amazing fashion show, I came upon a blurb that caught my eye. "Danielle Torrez, ex-wife of Red Sox pitcher Mike Torrez, and a successful Montreal model from the world-famous Jo Penney Agency, is putting some of her multi-million dollar alimony settlement into a self-titled modelling agency at the fashionable Vendome building on Newbury Street. She plans to start fielding offers from Boston's top public relations firms to handle her account."

The wheels started turning immediately.

I read the blurb out loud to Grant. "Dude, let's go work for this Danielle lady."

Grant looks at me. "Are you crazy? We don't know anything about models."

"We just did a killer fashion show," I said, "Plus, models are hotter than college girls and I'm tired of college girls."

The plan came together in my mind, in the words of my prep school headmaster George Bartlett "with the speed of summer lightning." *We'll call her, get a meeting, tell her that we're p.r. grad students, and that before she blows three hundred-K of her hard-earned money on retaining a firm, we'll handle her p.r. in-house!*

Simple.

He was skeptical, but said, "You get the meeting, I'll be there."

I called Information, got the number from our student office phone, asked for Ms. Torrez, and she came to the phone.

"Who are you and what do you want?" she said.

I said, "Hi, I'm Sarge, a masters grad student in public relations at Boston University, and I read in the *Herald* that you're about to retain a p.r. firm to handle your amazing new agency. Well, I'd like to save you tons of money."

"I'm listening."

"My partner and I would like to come share some of our ideas with you in person, and we guarantee that you will be the top modeling agency in Boston within six months or you can fire us on the spot."

She took a long pause. Then, "Do you know where I am?"

"Of course I do. We'll be there tomorrow morning. How's eleven?"

"I'll see you then." Click.

I called Grant. "Dude! Get your artist portfolio case! We have a meeting with the model agency tomorrow morning!"

The next day, we put on the only collared shirts we had, tied our only ties, and hopped the T to the Vendome. Grant sat nervously, fidgeting, and he kept whispering to me, "What are we gonna tell her? 'We aren't really grad students, we have no idea what we're doing, please hire us?' What are we gonna SAY?!"

I played it very cool. "Just sit there with your empty art portfolio case, smile and nod a lot, and let me do the talking."

I'd never done this before so I don't know where I got the confidence from, but I knew it would work. *I knew it.*

A few minutes later, Kathy, the lovely receptionist, told us Danielle Torrez was ready for us and we could go right in.

We walked in and were met by a stunning blonde in a crème colored Carolina Herrera day suit, reclining in her chair, angled with her back to the door, her sleek high heeled pumps up on the desk, tapping her fingertips together in confident contemplation. She stared out the window, not really acknowledging us directly.

"So. What can you do for me?" She asked pointedly, with a classic French-Montreal accent.

"We'll make your new little agency the top agency in Boston within six months, guaranteed."

"You said that on the phone. How do you plan to achieve this?"

I talked a mile-a-minute, ideas spilling out one after the other for how we would stage eye-popping events all over the city, raising public awareness, and even more importantly, INDUSTRY awareness, of her models, her agency, HER—without having any idea whatsoever how I would actually do it. I was a master of improvisation, even then, fueled by naiveté and confidence, with very little life experience. At twenty-one, I convinced everyone, including myself, that I was extremely self-motivated and confident. Ironic, given that my life would later degenerate into an existence of very little confidence, catastrophic self-hatred, and insecurity

"I'm very interested," she said, "How much do you two want to do this, to 'make me the top agency in Boston within six months' as you promise me?"

I paused briefly. Grant looked up at me. I looked back at him.

"Three hundred bucks a week," I blurted out, "Each."

We were undergrads and it was 1983, so three hundred bucks then was like asking for fifteen hundred today. She continued to stare out the window as though the answer was written on the side of one of the brownstone buildings in the alley. We held our breath. After what seemed like hours (probably thirty seconds or so), she turned and simply said, "Done. When do you start?"

"We already have," I said, "We're here, aren't we?"

Fresh from successfully staging ONE fashion event on campus, we were actually hired at a real live modeling agency. You could fit what Grant and I knew about promoting models in a thimble, but what we didn't have in real experience we made up for in *chutzpah*. It was sheer *chutzpah* to think we could get a meeting with Danielle in the first place, and more *chutzpah* to misrepresent ourselves, but the real *chutzpah* was never once considering even the possibility that we wouldn't be hired.

And with that, I effectively dropped out of a second college.

My parents didn't know—not about leaving school, not about my *loophole* money, not about anything really. They didn't know *me*. Who can blame them? I didn't know *me* either.

Grant and I started Monday with Danielle fulltime, and I was brimming with ideas, vowing that we'd do them all. My favorite was the one that created the most stir, and really got the phones ringing for the first time at the agency.

It was a bunch of fake fashion shoots.

I faked it. Nothing new, right?

We designed a huge white canvas banner with "Danielle" splashed across it in all the colors of the rainbow. It took us less than an hour to create on the floor of my apartment. We loaded the van with the first five models Danielle signed to the agency, a photographer, the newly created agency banner, and a couple of portable stanchions.

We pulled up in front of buildings all over town that housed Boston's biggest advertising agencies, unloaded and set up our fake photo shoots, complete with flashes going off, the photographer barking out directions to the models, and the agency signage as the backdrop. I patrolled around the edges handing out business cards for "Boston's Newest Modeling Agency, representing the HOTTEST MODELS IN THE WORLD." I had no idea if it would work. Often we were harassed and chased off by the cops for creating a disturbance. But that was the point. *We created a disturbance*—in front of the Hancock Building, Boston Commons, on the waterfront, in front of the Hines auditorium, on Newbury Street, in front of Neiman's. Wherever there was foot traffic, we'd park illegally and unload.

Who wouldn't want to watch gorgeous young girls modeling?

I was a college kid with raging hormones and it was cool to me, but apparently, it was also cool to the public, and *very* cool to everyone in the ad business. Phones started ringing off the hook: Photographers, ad agency casting people, art directors, models from other agencies, the Boston Police, *The Boston Globe*... Mission accomplished.

Shortly after we began, my pal Grant quit—for reasons I don't remember—maybe he wanted to go back and actually finish school—but I stayed. My friends back at Ad Lab haven't even figured out how to construct a resume, and I was the public relations director for a hot Boston modeling agency on fashionable Newbury Street. There I was, getting paid and having a ball. My one big disappointment, though, was however much I thought, *Yeah! MODELS! I'm gonna get laid!*

I thought wrong, but you can't blame a guy for trying.

Other promotions also went well, making it seem like I actually knew what I was doing. And yes: Danielle had the top modeling agency in Boston within six months of its opening. The buzz, the business, the models defecting from other agencies to come be with the *hot* agency. It was all happening in large part to the crazy college kid—me.

But too much attention is never enough.

I wanted to stage a fashion show, not just *any* fashion show, a sizzling, hot, *important* fashion show. I used the same basic premise as the college fashion show, where I got businesses and the community involved, but this time we booked the hottest venue, and had the hottest models. Of course, we didn't have to look far for a host and master of ceremonies this time either.

You know who.

I staged it at the Metro, on Lansdowne Street, where the homerun balls finally come down after they "hit 'em over the green monstaaah" at Red Sox games. I'd done a fashion show promotion before, but this time, it'd be REAL models, at a REAL night club and it would be for REAL. I had no way of knowing how real, but I organized the "Big Winter Go-See" at the Metro. (Go-see is a modeling industry term for when photographers, ad agencies and other booking buyers have models in for casting, hence, "go-see.")

I've always been lucky.

A group of big booking agents from the top agencies in New York happened to be in Boston for a confab at the same time. They saw the promotional posters for the event and thought it might be entertaining to attend, maybe even funny. They didn't expect much. But the models were phenomenal that night, in clothes from some of Boston's top fashion retailers, with hair and make-up by one of Newbury Street's most exclusive salons.

It wasn't just the event that was a smash that night. I was too. I got huge laughs as the host and master of ceremonies. Everyone saw me arrive in one of Danielle's Mercedes convertibles, in clothes she purchased especially for me for that night, since, as she insisted, "Nobody represents me in jeans."

After the show I was approached by several tipsy women, business cards in hand, wanting to meet this "Sarjay" whose name was listed in the program.

"Sarjay?" I asked, "Where do you see that?"

One of the women pointed at the last line of the program, Event Creator and Producer (titles I gave myself in the program) SARGE. For some reason they Frenched it up and thought they were looking for "Sarjay." I said, "I'm Sarjay, but it's pronounced SARGE?"

"So sorry, I'm so and so from Ford Models in New York." Another woman was from Elite Model Management. And there were more. They all seemed to be offering me a job, and they were all speaking simultaneously. On my right was a woman with curly dark brown hair, with a drink in one hand and one of those skinny brown cigarettes in the other. She said, "I'm Rona Siegel from Wilhelmina and you are FABULOUS. If you're ever in New York... that is, do you ever come to New York?"

Proud as punch, I said, "I'm FROM New York."

"Well if you ever want to come back and work for Wilhelmina, we'll train you and you'll be with THE agency."

There was no google in those days or any way of really looking things up or "vetting" anything, but these women seemed serious and out of all of them, I LOVED this Rona person.

A couple of months went by.

The bloom was starting to fade for me at Danielle. Once I created the initial pop that the agency enjoyed, she and her agency director began to take credit for all of the *fabulousness* of the agency and its meteoric rise from such a small startup.

I couldn't go back to school, because once I stopped going to classes and started working, they formally cut me from their rolls, and ultimately, I would never finish college.

I was also dating a local star model from another agency who I was head-over-heels in love with, Kate O'Connell. Well, in my mind we were dating. In hers? I guess we were just friends, since nothing ever materialized with her. We used to get stoned and play a game we called *Whack-a-Roach*—where we'd smoke a joint, turn off the lights in my roach-infested apartment, wait for the roaches to come out, then flick the lights back on again. As the roaches scrambled for cover we'd whack them with a hammer. Stoned, it was absolutely hilarious. Think about it sober, maybe not so much.

Kate was the top commercial print model in Boston at the time. Elite invited her to sign with them in New York, and I figured it was my chance too. I called Rona at Wilhelmina, quit Danielle Model Management, and followed Kate to New York.

NEW YORK CONNECTION

Rona arranged an interview with me at Wilhelmina as soon as I got to town. I met with her and with a woman named Karen Hilton, the women's division director. Karen was a plucky, fast-talking, animated woman with a boy's haircut. I was in love. They hired me on the spot and started training me on the Hollywood board. There were three models' schedule boards, A-K, L-Z, and Hollywood for the top models.

So there I was.
I hadn't finished college.
I'd run exactly two fashion shows.

And the Hollywood board, with all its complicated looking information, sat directly in front of me. It was a long wall-mounted countertop, with a wall of flip cards that held each model's schedule for the entire year, and a three-ring binder so stuffed with pages, you needed to be an Olympic heavy-lifter to pick it up.

How did I get here?

There was a woman on my right and two on my left, one of whom was Rona. I watched and listened day after day. Each phone had a little switch on the side and when you took a booking you flipped it, and a tape cassette device would record the information. The machine would often fail, so pad and pencil always needed to be handy. Bookers arranged general appointments, scheduled go-sees for castings, chit-chatted, cajoled, counseled, and *handled* models; careers.

I'm a Booker!

Bookers were one part booking agent, one part best friend and ten parts TMZ, thirty years before there was a TMZ. When you weren't answering the phones you were dialing them. Your bible was the List—private numbers of every photographer, art director, retail store fashion director, and catalog house in the world. By the time I left Wilhelmina, I knew every single phone number in that directory by heart. It was hard, hard work but it was so much fun. Every couple of hours or so, a model client would pop in with something fattening for *her* Booker, and for anyone else who wanted to continue to gain weight while sitting in a chair and running the model universe.

I was the only man in the office other than the co-owner, Bill Weinberg. The other owner was a barrel shaped woman named Fran Rothschild, who never smiled, except for when she'd say something nasty or caustic. She wore half-glasses all the time, and would seldom come out of the accounting office unless it was to set one foot outside her office and scowl at everyone in the booking office dismissively. It was rumored that she drove two hours in each direction from Holmdel, New Jersey every day through the most infuriating rush hour traffic. EVERY DAY. Her demeanor quite possibly could have been the byproduct of that drive. I thought she hated me, but Rona reassured me, "Fran hates everybody. And believe me, if Fran hated you, you'd be gone already."

Prophetic words indeed.

One day, all of the other women on my board had either gone to lunch or the loo. The phone rang and I answered.

"Good afternoon, Wilhelmina, can I help you?"

The voice on the other end wasn't familiar to me, nowhere near as familiar as it would soon be to everyone on the planet.

"Baby, this is Whit, and I need to book out for four months."

That meant that for four months she didn't want to be booked for anything.

I found her schedule card. "Hey Whit," I said, "You really want to book out for four months? You have piles of confirmed bookings here." I'd been trained to take bookings but had never encountered anyone that wanted to *cancel* them. "Forgive me for asking, but why do you want to cancel all of these bookings?"

"Oh, I'm sorry baby, I didn't tell you I'm working on an album?"

I laughed to myself. "An ALBUM. What kind of ALBUM?"

"A music album, I'm a singer."

"A singer? Hold on a second, Whit."

I was alone on the board and the other veteran bookers hadn't come back yet, and I said out loud to myself, "Another model that thinks she's gonna be a singer, what a moron."

Rona came back from the bathroom right then,

"Who are you talking to?"

I rolled my eyes. "Another fucking model who wants to be a singer, and she wants to cancel four months of CONFIRMED bookings to do it."

She looked at the phone bank and frantically asked me, "Where is she? That's Whitney Houston!" *Whitney who?*

"She's on hold," I said.

Rona looked at all of the phones. "No one's on hold. Wait. Your phone isn't fully in the cradle."

She was right.

Whitney Houston was not on hold. She was still on the line. And she heard EVERY SINGLE WORD I SAID.

Rona picked up the line and tried to do damage control, "Yes girl, no girl, he was kidding, he's new." About an hour later I saw the icon we would all come to know—a tall, beautiful African-American woman in a fur coat and shades, looking like the character she would play a few years later in *The Bodyguard*, making her way off the elevator into Fran's office. I thought nothing of it until Fran emerged from her office and gestured to me to come to her.

"Take lunch and don't come back. I'll send you your check."

Another fucking model who wants to be a singer.

That album catapulted Whitney Houston to superstardom, sold twenty five million copies worldwide, and had three number one singles.

Another fucking model who wants to be a singer.

Oops. Maybe I deserved what I got.

Ironically, Whitney suffered from alcoholism and drug addiction—as we all later learned—the same disease that I've been fortunate enough to recover from. Like everyone else, I watched in horror as her life spiraled downward. I was given the tools to stop that madness from destroying me, and somehow, for me, it worked. There but for the grace of God.

After being unceremoniously dumped by Wilhelmina, I needed to find a job. I had thousands of phone numbers still in my head, but I was in shock from the firing, so I drank.

Every night.

I piggybacked from my college recreational daily pot smoking career to drinking seriously. I didn't drink just anywhere though. I had an Amex card and a decent income (before I was fired). My favorite restaurant was Canastel's, a Northern Italian gourmet spot popular with models and "model humpers" alike, owned by the legendary proprietor of The Herald Square Diner, Mark Packer. It was in the recently renovated Park Avenue South area in Manhattan, and Canastel's was THE place to hang if you were in the advertising, photography, or modeling industry. As a modeling agent, I went there four nights a week. My drink of choice was scotch, a vile guzzling alcohol, but I'd order a triple and guzzle it like I was rehydrating. Canastel's was always nine deep at the bar while people waited for their tables, though lots of people drank and did so much cocaine in the bathroom, they never actually ate.

One night while I was drinking in the crush of thirsty people, I was talking to someone, and another woman was literally back up against me. She said to me over her shoulder, "Your voice sounds so familiar, you wouldn't be Steven from Wilhelmina would you?"

"That's right."

"I'm Kate Sciotto from Nobart," she said excitedly. Nobart was a catalog production studio in New York that booked dozens of models from Wilhelmina.

"Nobart! No shit! You're Kate? I talk to you every day, WOW, amazing, you don't look anything like your voice!"

We commiserated. I told her my story about leaving Wilhelmina, and she told me hers about leaving Nobart. And it turned out that though she had been working at an agency called HV Models, running their men's division, she'd recently been offered an opportunity to run a new agency with a guy named Mark Grossich, who owned an advertising agency and public relations firm...

And they were looking for a third partner to run a woman's division!

I imagined Kate Sciotto must have thought of me as quite a Booker to offer me the possibility. WOW. Not just a job, but a PARTNERSHIP? I took her number.

"Call me tomorrow. You will call?" she asked.

"Are you kidding?"

The next day I called.

"So were you drunk, or would you still like to meet?" I asked.

"When can you be here?"

"I'm on my way over."

I met with Kate and her partner Mark and they offered me a salary plus a third of the net profits. I was twenty-four. Twenty-four years-old, and I would be an owner of a high fashion representation firm in the epicenter of fashion representation. Once again, I had lucked my way into a situation that I had no previous experience in, but ballsy as ever, I knew that I could do what needed to be done.

We called the agency Punch.

For some reason I was supremely confident.

I had to put a modeling agency woman's division together from scratch. Thank God for the senior agents at Wilhelmina, Gina Savarese, Ginni Samardge, Karen Lucarelli, Karen Hilton and of course, Rona Siegel. They gave me a priceless education in putting model portfolios together, making appointments, and negotiating bookings. Plus, I already had the whole industry phone list in my head.

Another very important thing I learned from the agents at Wilhelmina was to respect the clients and treat them respectfully—*another fucking model* notwithstanding.

I was a straight man doing a gay man's job. Most straight men who are around models all the time are in it for sex, or for the hope of sex. Don't get me wrong, I would have liked to have had more dalliances in connection with the *professionally pretty*, but it wasn't like they were chasing ME around the desk and I still really didn't have any experience with women. I was also terrified of them.

I was up to my eyebrows, surrounded by beautiful women, but my social fear was overwhelming. It's the same fear that got me drinking and taking drugs. *I'm not enough. I'm nothing.* I thought I was fat and unattractive, and I felt terminally confused on the inside.

Actually, I had a lot in common with the models, who often suffered from the same fears. They starved. I ate. But it was all the same. For me, though, my weight was the thing that sealed the deal—I wasn't just shameful, I was *gross* and unable to compete with more attractive men.

My guy friends thought I was getting laid all the time, they just *assumed*. After all, I was the one in the model business. And I did nothing to dissuade them. I liked people thinking I was sleeping with beautiful models. As long as people thought I was getting laid, I didn't mind that I wasn't. What people thought of me was so important. But if anyone knew how driven by shame I was, they would not have believed it, because I appeared to be so on top of things and confident.

It's hard for even me to understand.

In a way, I *was* confident. Confident that I could get models work, confident of how to sell them to buyers, and confident that I would be successful. Hell, I RAN an agency. But underneath, I was deeply unconfident that I mattered at all to anyone—or that I ever would. I was still the little boy who no one believed, who didn't know for sure where he came from or what he was.

In just a few months in business and we were killing it. Models were flocking from top agencies to be repped by Punch. Okay, so no *supermodels*, but viable, representable ladies with good portfolios who were the right height for runway shows, the right look for commercial print, and the right type for television commercials. These were the gradients for being represented, but my partners and I believed that if you made enough phone calls, if you pushed hard enough, you could find a modeling job for a shaved German Shepherd.

"Burn the phones and the phone lines will burn up!" Mark said to us constantly. He was mostly right, but there were a thousand variables and components that went into a successful agency. He and Kate worked hard, but truth be told, the women's division was the lifeblood of Punch. In those days, maybe still, there was a hugely disproportionate amount of modeling work for women and comparatively little for men. Aside from Marky Mark for Calvin Klein and the Perry Ellis guy in all the magazines, there were maybe fifty male models in New York making real bank. Punch Models had only one of those fifty guys. My division, however, the *women*—well, that was a whole other story. There was TONS of work for the ladies.

I got them the modeling jobs and Punch began to grow and grow.

We worked twelve-hour days and then partied for the other twelve hours. Many nights I'd swing home after partying all night, stop at my loft apartment on 30th Street, shower, change, and go right back into the office to do it all over again.

You can sleep when you're dead. And it's always Happy Hour somewhere. The modeling business is perfect for addicts. If the appetite to consume intoxicants is present, there is absolutely no shortage of places to satisfy that appetite, and we could get in anywhere, just by making a call.

"No, we're not WITH Punch Models. We ARE Punch Models."

We were always on the List.

I was using cocaine all the time at this point and still didn't have even the beginning of an inkling that it might be a problem. I liked the way it made me feel. I'm an energetic, hyper person anyway, though, so the higher high made me drink more. What a combo. The problem with coke was that it was expensive—and I absolutely could not do without it.

But I wasn't addicted, right?

Everyone in the modeling business had cocaine in the mid-80s—hell, it seemed like everyone in New York in EVERY business. I OWNED a modeling agency, I was a partner. *I deserved cocaine.* Reagan's *War on Drugs* may have effectively slowed the flow of marijuana into New York to a trickle, but somehow practically ALL of the coke slipped through the DEA's net. Everyone had it. Everyone did it. I think about that now. *Really? Everybody?* Well, everyone I hung wanted to be around did. Maybe that says it all right there.

I wasn't interested in knowing people who didn't do drugs.

I wasn't interested in being with occasional partiers who knew when to stop and never let it interfere with their *real* lives.

I wanted escape. I wanted cocaine. Period.

And even though I was making a lot of money, my habit was outstripping my ability to pay for it. I never saw a boundary I didn't want to crash through, or a line I didn't want to cross.

I coerced one of our Punch clients into fronting the money for one of my larger drug buys. Now she wanted the money back. She was serious, and she was *pissed*—threatening to go to the media.

But I didn't have the money to pay her back.

My partners, Kate and Mark knew that the story would be juicy fodder for any one of a number of television magazine shows, who were fascinated by the seamier side of the modeling industry. *Drug overdoses! Anorexia and bulimia! Wild sex!* And now, potentially, an owner in a respected agency using his position of power to get a poor, defenseless model to buy him drugs.

I don't know how poor or defenseless she was, but they knew

that was how it would be painted. How Punch would be painted. How *they* would be painted.

They bought me out.

I was done.

But it still didn't occur to me that my toxic appetite for cocaine had anything to do with the *unfairness* and the *bad luck* that was dogging me. As far as I was concerned, everything that happened was someone else's fault—better to pretend like it didn't matter and move on to the next adventure.

There would always be a next adventure.

I decided I was tired of making other people stars. I was a hit as an emcee, on the phones, in meetings. *Everyone said so.* Why not become a star myself? I applied to the Lee Strasberg Theater Institute. The woman who signed me in told me I didn't have a prayer—there were hundreds of other applicants, all with more experience and/or prior training, and the Institute was only accepting twelve new students.

"Those rules don't apply to ME." I said it right out. She was unimpressed. But I was right. I prepared my monologue, knocked it out of the park, and I was accepted.

For many addicts, the belief that rules don't apply to them is a kind of delusion. Sure, they can con friends and loved ones out of money or drugs, but the feelings of omnipotence and power are largely drug-fueled and imaginary. It was my tragedy at that time in my life, as cocaine was taking over, that I really *did* often bend the world to my will. I had a laundry list of times the rules didn't apply to me, with the money and success to prove it wasn't bullshit.

So much money. So much that I had to get a model to buy drugs for me. *So much success.* So much that I was forced out of my own company even though I was instrumental in making it such a success. That's the weird Catch 22 of addiction. Everything my mind told me was true. But everything my mind told me was also a lie. I could make miracles and turn them into shit.

So sure, I beat the odds and got into the Lee Strasberg Institute. For what? I remember almost nothing of my initial ten weeks there and I wasted the opportunity. I still had my Punch Models corporate credit card, and continued to drink every night at Canastel's after acting class. I was into pink champagne. *Pink Champagne!?* I threw parties constantly in my gigantic loft apartment, usually with over a hundred people, and room for more—you could actually stand up in the fireplace the apartment was so big. That was some joint.

But soon, without any income at all, and with very little of the buyout left, I would live in increasingly diminished circumstances, with a series of sublet and roommate situations all over Manhattan. *Yorkville, Greenwich Village, lower Manhattan.* I was on my way to homelessness and I didn't even know it.

One night, still pretending everything was fine, I ran into a guy that knew who I was from the model agency business. He told me he was working with some people who were looking for someone who could help them with a computerized casting system. *Computers! So futuristic!* The idea was to give everyone in print, television commercials, and movies the ability to cast for very specific needs by keying in some basic details. If you needed a six-foot redhead with a black belt in karate, who could ride a horse and speak Latvian, you could find her with a few keystrokes.

It was called *Starkives*. You know, like *archives*. But with stars.

They had a slick promotional commercial shot with Joe Montana, Kathy Lee Crosby, Linda Evans, and Kenny Rogers endorsing the product and confirming their involvement. I'd later find out that Starkives was the brainchild of industry mogul John Casablancas of Elite Model Management, however, no one could know he was involved because if other agencies found out, they wouldn't take part. For a casting system like this to become a comprehensive tool, it was essential for all of the big four agencies to be on board—Ford, Click,

Elite, and Wilhelmina.

The system was really quite ingenious. Pioneer had just invented the laser disc—basically a CD the size of a vinyl record that could hold up to fifty-four thousand still images. There were a lot of models in the world, but hardly that many.

In the '80s, one of the costliest pieces of the modeling agency expense pie was still sending clunky, heavy portfolios in for consideration EVERY TIME there was a potential booking, casting, or job. Whether sending a bunch of books to Midtown, or to Paris, messenger fees and shipping fees were astronomical, costing the models and the agencies millions of dollars annually.

Starkives would enable buyers to find talent right at their desks, with the discs updated monthly. To start, all subscribers needed was a Pioneer Laser Disc player and the first Starkives disc. But *someone* had to get ALL the modeling agencies to sign up for the prototype and magically of course that *someone* was me.

While I was brainstorming with myself about this awesome new job and the task at hand, I thought, what if we also approached the top photographers in the fashion business, and all of the make-up and hair stylists to put portfolio samples of their work on the system as well. Fifty-four thousand images meant a lot of work for all the art directors, creative directors, hell, anyone in the business of conceiving, shooting, appearing in, or creating advertising. What if we got them involved too? More people, more money, and wider acceptance in the industry. It was a natural. My new bosses went for it, and I set out to make it a reality. I set appointments with Joey and Francis Grill at CLICK, Ford Models, and Wilhelmina's Bill Weinberg, whose partner Fran had fired me just one year earlier. It was the right idea at the right time. No one wanted to be left out—they could save tons of money *and* gain an edge in the extremely competitive fashion industry—and every important agency threw open their books, assigning top agents from their offices, and giving me carte blanche and editorial control.

I was the *expert*, right?

I kept to the bargain, and never once mentioned Elite or John Casablanca being behind the enterprise—actually they were the last of the big four that I met with the pitch the prototype. That they signed on was not exactly a surprise.

My access broadened, and I found myself at photographers' studios that were so major, they wouldn't even take my calls back when I was just another Booker. Now they were answering to me. I had to pinch myself to see if I was even alive. *Richard Avedon, Patrick Demarchlier, Patrice Casanova, Bill King, Albert Watson...* They gave me access to their cherished laminated photos and tear sheets. (A tear sheet is an original of published work from magazines and other media that a model, photographer, or creative uses to create his or her portfolio.)

It came together very, very quickly and I worked seven days a week until the prototype disc was ready to be mastered. The mastering went smoothly, the menu-driven Pioneer system was easy to operate and it *worked*. Starkives was a reality.

First problem:

If Starkives was going to make itself ubiquitous throughout the industry, literally *thousands* of end users—everyone in the business of hiring models—needed a Pioneer Laser Disc Player. And they had no incentive to purchase the players on their own, because the old way of bringing in bulky portfolio books worked fine for them, because it cost them NOTHING. They could request dozens of books before deciding on one model, while bearing none of the costs of maintaining or delivering the books.

So the system would only work if Starkives purchased and supplied those thousands of Pioneer Laser Disc Players.

Second problem:

The people behind Starkives—some with mob ties—had spent all of the company's seed investment on Yankee tickets, limousines, and other extravagances that had nothing to do with making the operation successful. It was fraud. We had the product that could revolutionize the modeling industry, but we had no money to push it over the finish line. I showed up to work one day and the office I'd been working in next to Grand Central Station was locked and boarded up, with an FBI sticker on the glass doors.

Starkives 1.0 was dead.

That was until one night at Studio 54. That's right, I'm old enough to have partied at Studio 54, or *Studio*, as it was known. I met a lecherous little olive-colored man with a silk ascot and cigarette holder named Phillippe De Montpeyroux, who recognized me from a top photographer's studio party. Phillippe was a male model chaser and claimed to be a marquis from France. (I later learned he was actually an outcast from Tunisia who just *spoke* French.) He had heard about Starkives, and was very interested in acquiring the prototype.

He wanted to bring me to meet his partner Gregoire.

Phillippe and Gregoire. I was going international, with no time to sink into a druggy haze at racking up another failure—since Starkives might still have a chance. Phillippe said Gregoire was a *billionaire*, and the fiancée of Virginia Warner, Senator John Warner's daughter, who was also the granddaughter of the Mellon family of Mellon Bank.

He asked me if I wanted to be rich.

I was young, broke, and jobless.

Yes. I want to be rich.

The next day I was told to go to 45th Street and Fifth Avenue to a storefront called Manhattan Electronics. I was supposed to ask for *The Boss*. Very cloak and dagger. So bright and early I made my way over to Manhattan Electronics—a retail warehouse of wires, cables, and connectors. I asked for *The Boss*, and was taken upstairs, through the back, to a service elevator.

I was so naïve—but thrilled and excited—*I was gonna be rich!*

The owners behind Starkives were in whatever legal trouble they were in, but I had done all the work collecting the images and information, and I had the prototype disc.

Possession is nine tenths of the law.

Plus I needed to save face with an entire industry of modeling agency owners, top photographers, and buyers.

I didn't care if I was in the service elevator of a dodgy electronics warehouse. This was my chance to make everything right.

Down a long, shabby hallway, I was led to an office, where a tall, skinny *barefoot* man sat at a desk piled high with papers, cigar cutters, and empty espresso cups. He had sunken cheeks, bad hair plugs, and his pants were open. A demitasse cup was in one hand and a cigar in the other, and he was screaming in French at a speaker phone. The voice coming from the other end was unintelligible but the hair plug guy seemed to be in command of the conversation. Finally he bellowed, "Fuuuuuuuuuck!" and the call was over.

Not skipping a beat, he turned to me, extended his hand, and smiled widely.

"Boss!" he chortled, "Boss! You're here!"

Then he kissed both sides of my face. He reeked from a mixture of expensive cologne, cigars, and coffee.

This was Gregoire De Rothschild.

"Sit down! Sit down, Boss," he commanded. "I'm going to hire you, Boss, you're beautiful, Boss, you're a genius, Boss, I want you to be rich, I want to give you money, I love you, Boss."

Well, this was going well.

I wasn't the least bit skeptical. What was wrong with me? If you google this guy right now, Aaron Berdah, a.k.a. Gregoire De Rothschild, you'll find dozens of fraud, money laundering, and extortion charges, brought from the New York State Supreme Court all the way to Switzerland, for among other things, misrepresenting himself as a banker and as an heir to the Rothschild fortune.

But we didn't have google yet. We barely had computers.

"How much do you want, Boss?"

"I don't know, twelve hundred a week?"

He went into the pocket of his now falling down suit pants and threw down an ATM card.

"GO! Go to the bank machine on the corner and withdraw your paycheck, Boss." He gave me his pin code and told me to go before he changed his mind."

He gave me the office next door to his, and I went to work resurrecting the recently comatose project that I'd worked day and night for five months to create. *Starkives would live!*

On the third day of my employment, Gregoire invited me into his office for some espresso. I obliged and while he was making the espresso shots he asked me if I wanted some *Oooooot.*

"Oooooot? What's that?"

"Coke, Boss, cocaine."

I actually hesitated, if you can believe it. But even I had some standards. I was at work, just starting a new job.

Gregoire went into a box on his desk, pulled out a little shelf from the side, and began to chop up coke with the same ATM card that I'd used only days before to withdraw my salary. I took a sip of the espresso. It was bitter and horrible. I drank it down.

"Boss, come on, Boss, it's the best *Oooooot.*"

I did a line off the desk shelf and my integrity and dignity went right out the window as the coke went up my nose. I did it in my office. I did it at Gregoire's apartment. As a matter of fact I had no place to live at that time, so I did coke as I slept on the floor of his living room, incidentally, lying right next to, and sharing a pillow with, Phillippe, the *marquis,* who had introduced us.

I was so busy using cocaine and being a slave to my addiction, it never occurred to me to ask why this supposed French marquis didn't have an apartment of his own, or even his own pillow.

The rest of the Starkives 2.0 story is lost. It never really got off the ground, but I don't remember how or why. A cloud of coke obscures the events that followed.

I did so much blow.

I hate to sound like a crook hauled before a Senate sub-committee to testify, but *I do not recall* anything other than what I've shared so far. I was an addict, though I still refused to acknowledge the fact. Days rushed by in a blur, fueled by cocaine and espresso, as I worked for fraudsters and conmen, getting paid in cash—hell, I'm surprised it wasn't counterfeit. For all I know, maybe it was.

I was cocaine's bitch.

Amazingly enough, I still had four more years to go before I actually hit rock bottom. It took four more years of crazy highs and even crazier lows to bring me to my knees.

It took what it took, I guess.

Meanwhile I drifted.

I was finished in the modeling business, but I had no particular focus—no bright ideas. I did odd jobs, worked for friends, and I kept getting high.

HIGH IN THE WIDE WORLD OF SPORTS

It was June of 1989.

My beloved Mets had won the World Series in 1986 and with the amazing team they had, should have won in '87, '88, and '89. I may have had no real career focus, but the Mets still commanded my attention.

Maybe I'll become a baseball play-by-play announcer...?

I'd been listening to games on the radio practically since I was born. How hard could announcing be? You watch the game and tell the listeners what you see on the field. Not exactly brain surgery.

I figured it was like models looking for voice over work, and that I'd need a demo tape if I wanted an announcer's job in Major League Baseball.

With a fresh supply of AA batteries and a cheap hand-held Sony cassette recorder in hand, I went out to Shea Stadium on the subway, and recorded my own play-by-play of the game. I don't remember too much about the game except that Darryl Strawberry, Howard Johnson, and Kevin McReynolds hit back-to-back-to-back home runs. I was on the first base side behind the dugout *doing the game* into my little Sony cassette recorder. I must have seemed like a total lunatic to everyone around me—and I must have been VERY annoying.

I took the tape home, and for weeks I just played it for friends— I didn't take any concrete steps to put my plan into action. Finally, a buddy of mine asked, "Dude, it sounds just like the radio. Why don't you send it to someone at Major League Baseball. *Simple.*"

Right. But where would I start? THEN IT HIT ME. *Why not just call the Major League Baseball Commissioner directly?* I'd ask him to listen to my homemade demo tape and ask for his help. Most people would say I was crazy, but, sometimes the craziest ideas turn out to be the best ones. So, I called directory assistance and got the number of Major League Baseball.

"Hello. Major League Baseball."

"Yes, I'd like to speak to the Commissioner please."

"Hold on. Connecting."

"Good Morning, Commissioners office, can I help you?"

"May I please speak to the Commissioner? My name is Steven Pickman and today's my birthday." (It actually WAS my birthday, by the way, I wasn't playing an angle.)

"It's my birthday, and I've decided to become a sportscaster. I'm willing to start at the bottom and I'm willing to do anything—"

The woman on the other end of the line in the Commissioner's office cut me off.

"Whoa, whoa, whoa, slow down. First of all, is it REALLY your birthday?"

"Of course it is."

"Happy Birthday." She continued, "Unfortunately, the Commish is out of town at the moment on MLB business. But since it's your birthday, I'm going to leave something for you at the reception desk of our office."

Really!?

"But you can't tell anyone where you got it. I'm serious."

I would have agreed to anything, any terms, though I still had no idea what she was planning to give me.

"What is it that I can't tell anyone anything about?" I asked.

"You'll see. Do you have our address?"

"I know where you are—and thanks a BUNCH for— *whatever* it is that I'm thanking you for!"

I put on pants, hopped in a cab, and went over to 245 Park Avenue, where—GET THIS—I went directly into the building, into the elevators, and directly to the reception desk, without being x-rayed, MRI'd, frisked, or rubber-glove searched like I was on the no-fly list. I stepped up to the counter and said to the woman feverishly fielding incoming calls, "Hi. I'm Steven 'Sarge' Pickman, and I believe there's something here for me?"

"One moment please. Ahhhhhh yes. This was just left for you by the commissioner's assistant."

She handed it to me. I didn't have to show my passport or my social security card or leave a stool sample. It was a crisp white, number ten envelope, with the embossed logo of Major League Baseball on the upper left hand corner. In raised letters underneath *THE COMMISSIONER OF BASEBALL*. I took it as though I were on some sort of official business and bolted out of there.

Once I was on the elevator, I carefully opened the envelope without disturbing the integrity of that cool logo. Folded inside were three or four pages, still warm from the Xerox machine. As I opened the folded pages I couldn't believe my eyes. They were copies of Rolodex cards, laid out in alphabetical order by company, ABC, BBC, CBS, etc., and each card had the names, addresses and DIRECT PHONE EXTENSIONS of all of the top executives in network television.

I had the names and numbers of them all in my stoned little hands.

I got back to my sublet, got naked, sparked a joint and looked over the list. (At this point in my addiction, I always liked getting high in the nude. It was my thing.) First up ABC. I dialed them up.

A man answered. "Yes?"

"Good afternoon, my name is Sarge, it's my birthday, I'm a very funny guy, I've decided that I want to be a sportscaster, and I'm willing to start at the bottom, mop floors if need be."

He chuckled. "C'mon, who is this really?"

I repeated my spiel. "It's Sarge, I'm funny, it's my birthday, I wanna sportscast, I'm ready to mop."

"You're serious, aren't you," he said, "Is it really your birthday?"

"Yes, it is."

"Well... Happy Birthday. Where did you go to school?"

"Boston."

I consciously avoided indicating whether it was Boston College or Boston University because of how easy it would be to check on my lack of completeness in the college degree area.

"Well," he said, "I wish I could help you, but I don't really do the hiring around here."

"Oh," I said, "Well, what do you do?"

"I kinda run the whole network, I'm Roone Arledge."

I was such an idiot. I didn't even know that I was talking to a MEDIA GIANT, and just said, "Great to meet you, Roone, so who does do the hiring?"

"I'll put you through to the guy," he said, "You tell him exactly what you told me, and best of luck." There was a clicking and a couple of rings, then another man answers.

"Sports."

"Hello, Sports," I said, and repeated my spiel. *Sarge, birthday, sportscasting, willing to mop...*

"Who is this?" he asked.

"Who is THIS?" I replied.

"I'm Jim O'Hara. How did you get my number? Is this a joke?"

"I assure you sir, this is not a joke," I said with all the earnest authority I could muster, "I just got off the phone with Roone, and he connected me to you."

"You just got off the phone with Roone did you? Well, Happy Birthday, first of all, but I don't hire the on-air people. Let me connect you with the guy who does. Good luck Sarge."

And another guy, and another guy.

Same spiel until the fifth guy, Tony Tortorici. He didn't wish me Happy Birthday and transfer me to someone else.

"Who exactly have you spoken to?" he asked.

"Roone and Jim and Moe and Larry and Curly," I said, "And now I'm on with you."

"Well, if you spoke to all of those guys, I guess I have to hire you," he said nonchalantly, "Where are you going to be this weekend?"

"Around," I said, determined to sound just as nonchalant.

"Great," he said, "Come to Atlantic City, take Amtrak, keep your receipts, there'll be a room for you at Trump Plaza. Meet us by the production trucks at noon Saturday."

"Okay," I said, "See you there."

Just like that.

Five phone calls, Roone Arledge, Jim O'Hara, and I'm working for ABC Sports. I knew it was amazing, but I don't know if I completely understood that it was a MIRACLE. *Well, it WAS my birthday...*

I set out early on Saturday and took the train to Atlantic City, walked from the train station to Trump Plaza. Next to it was the Atlantic City Convention Center, and right in front, the ABC Sports production trucks were lined up, ominous and cool looking, like huge white moving trucks with the famous ABC Sports logo on the side.

Cool.

I was an hour early and there was no one around except for a guy named Stu who was laying down cable. "Fiber optic phone lines," he told me.

"I'm the new hire," I said, unsure what I was supposed to do.

He offered me a seat on the oblong Igloo cooler outside of one of the trucks and I sat down to wait for whomever or whatever was going to happen next. About an hour later, three men in alligator shoes and khakis arrived carrying briefcases, like the waspy FBI. The one walking slightly ahead of the others asked me, "Are you the new guy?"

"Yes," I quickly answered. "Tony hired me Thursday after I spoke to Roone." I affected a sort of bantering tone, unaware that I was *bantering* with a legendary director and producer of sports television, Bob Goodrich. I thought throwing in that, *I spoke to Roone,* would help me in some way. *What an idiot.*

Bob Goodrich reached into his pocket and pulled out car keys with a crisp hundred dollar bill. "Get the car, it's a burgundy Sedan De

Ville in the lot over there, go to the White House, and get us some lunch."

"Isn't that a bit far to go for lunch," I said, "I mean, Washington D.C.?"

He laughed. "Smartass. The White House Sub Shop on Arctic Avenue. If you have a problem with anyone, here, show them this."

With that, he took a lanyard from around his neck with a laminated card attached that had the *Wide World of Sports* and ABC logos printed on it.

"Put this on, and everyone will know who you are."

Everyone'll know who I am!

Okay. I took the car key and started to bolt. My first real live ABC assignment, and I was gonna knock it out of the park. I got about ten feet from the men, and Goodrich called over, "Aren't you gonna take our orders?"

"Oh yes, what will it be gentlemen."

Goodrich answered for everyone. "Two with everything, one with extra onions and well done, extra cheese on mine, jalapenos on the side, and a bunch of cokes."

"Perfect," I said, "I gotcha."

"Aren't you gonna write this down?"

"Naaaaaah," I said, "I got it all up here."

I got about thirty yards away when I realized I had no idea what I was actually supposed to get for them from the White House on Arctic Avenue. I knew it was two with everything, one with extra onions, and the rest of it, but *everything* and *extra onions* on WHAT? Shit. I wasn't going back to ask, so I'd just have to figure it out once I got to the sub shop.

I found the White House, which was easy enough, because Atlantic City is divided into just two parts. One is luxurious and flashy with casinos. The other part looks like Syria on the evening news—desolate, bombed-out, and disastrous. After blocks and blocks of burned-out store fronts, scary rowhouses, and drug dealers on every corner that even I wouldn't have trusted, I found the White House. There was a line of folks out the door and around the block. At first I panicked. No wonder they sent me, this is gonna take hours. But once I parked and walked towards the place, a guy in the doorway with a clipboard, a host of sorts, saw the ABC credential hanging from my neck and motioned with his pen toward me.

"C'mere."

I walked over.

"You workin' on boxing?"

He pointed to my credential. I noticed the little boxing gloves next to the other logos.

"Uhhhhhhhh, yeah."

Actually, until that moment, I had no idea what we were in Atlantic City covering. But I was IN, ahead of everyone else. And the big thing everyone was eating was cheese steaks. I figured cheese steaks had to be what I was supposed to get with *everything* and *extra onions*. So, cheese steaks in hand, I headed back to the trucks. The sandwiches were huge, and I laid them out on a table outside the trucks, and went inside to let them know I was back. Goodrich herded them all out and started handing out sandwiches. Everyone was ecstatic, because they KNEW the culinary awesomeness they were about to partake in. I, of course, did not.

"Jalapenos, where are the jalapenos?"

"On the side," I said, "Like you asked."

I got every single order right, remembered every variation, even though I didn't even know that I was supposed to get cheese steaks.

"Great job, Son," he said, "I knew you were more than a lunch boy." For the first time that day, I knew my job description for *ABC Wide World of Sports*. I was the lunch boy. Okay. Two days before, I was unemployed, desperate to be a sportscaster, with a homemade demo tape and no idea what to do with it. Now I'm the lunch boy for

Sarge

ABC Sports. Rome wasn't built in a day. *Jim* Rome? That's a whole other story.

There was one cheese steak left. I reached for it nervously, unsure if I was actually authorized to have bought one for myself. As I pulled it from the bag, I heard Goodrich. "You got one for yourself, I see," he said. "Well dig in, we have work to do."

Then he looked at me.

"Where's my change? Where's the receipt? Are you trying to keep my money?"

He was completely deadpan. I looked at him and then at the other men's faces and for what seemed like five minutes. Finally, they all broke out laughing. I pretended not to be spooked.

"I had you going there for a second, huh?" he said.

"Yeah," I responded carefully, "You had me there for a second."

I gave him his change and the receipt.

I also learned that I wasn't officially the lunch boy—I was a *runner*. As a runner on boxing coverage, I had to learn the names and locations on-site of all essential personnel. That first event was a whirl of names and faces. I couldn't have gotten through it without Bobby Yalen—the network matchmaker who put the bouts together to create compelling matchups for the broadcast. He was as nice as he was important—down to earth, gentle, and kind. Odd for a man integral to creating televised savagery. Bobby took me everywhere with him, introduced me like I belonged, and clued me in about what I needed to know for my job.

That day and many, many days that followed, I could ask Bobby the dumbest questions, and he answered like a patient elementary school teacher. Like there were no stupid questions. He made me feel instantly comfortable. Because of his mentorship and kindness, I was hired back week after week on various coverages for ABC. He basically took me under his wing throughout the tenuous times of being a per diem employee of an ominously well-oiled machine like

ABC Wide World of Sports. I am eternally grateful the universe put Bobby Yalen in my path.

As I continued working for ABC, Goodrich usually had me working right on the shoulder of the announcers for the fights. Alex Wallau and Dan Dierdorf were the talent on the broadcast and I was assigned to them all day to get them whatever they needed—lunch, a beverage, notes from the researchers on the telecast, whatever—I was their guy. They were a little more stressed than Yalen because they were on-the-air while he was behind the scenes. And I was right there with them, one inch from being on camera at ringside. In my mind, I was THAT CLOSE to being a sportscaster on-the-air myself. Ridiculously, I actually thought if one of them came down with sudden laryngitis ringside, I'd be in the signature yellow jacket calling the fight.

Was I ever really that young?

A couple of weeks after I started, we were back in Atlantic City. Mike Tyson was in training for the Carl "The Truth" Williams fight and Alex Wallau was set to interview Tyson after his training session. I'd been ingratiating myself with the crew, entertaining them with my flawless impression of Tyson, lisp and all. They sent me to go get Mike and bring him to the interview.

I walked down to the hotel ballroom where "Tyson was doing sit-ups on a table with a handler holding his ankles, shouting out the count. *Three hundred forty-five, forty-six, forty-seven...* The air was electric. His entourage milled about in track suits with towels over their shoulders. Tyson was enormous—thick, wide, HUGE. I watched in amazement as he kept doing his sit-ups. I'd been told to find someone named Rory. I walked over to one of the entourage.

"Is Rory around?"

I referenced my ABC credential. The guy pointed me to the very table where Tyson was pumping out like his five hundredth sit-up. I guess Rory was the one holding Tyson's ankles. I was in awe of Mike Tyson, but I didn't envy Rory his job.

Sarge

I approached them gingerly.

"I'm with ABC and Alex is ready for Mike."

Tyson looked at me a little ticked off, like I was interrupting something important, and I swear to God, I absolutely froze.

"Just step back from the champ," said Rory evenly, "And I'll meet you over by the ring." Instead of coming with me for the interview, Tyson started jumping rope on the far side of the ballroom. I wasn't going to stop him. I wasn't going anywhere *near* him.

Finally, Rory came over and introduced himself.

"Hey man, I'm Rory, what's your name?"

I don't know what came over me. Nerves? Terror? Insanity? But I answered Rory in Tyson's voice. I'm meeting the man for the first time, I work for ABC, and I'm MOCKING MIKE TYSON. Some people are ballsy. Some crazy. I was both.

"I'm the nastiest man on the planet," I lisped, "I'm a disaster, I'm your master, I'll drive your nose into your brain."

Flawless Tyson impression. Rory took a step back, doubled over holding his nose with his index finger and thumb and said, "Dude! That is *awesome*! That's the best *Mike* I've ever heard anyone do!"

Suddenly I was struck by the insanity of what I'd just done.

"Please, don't tell him, please don't say anything," I begged.

"Nah," he said, "It's aiiiiight, I feel you man, I won't say anything."

He lied.

When Tyson was finally done with his workout, and Rory went over to put the now signature *white towel with a head hole in the middle* on Mike, his whole group walked towards me. Twelve or thirteen in all, like a swarm they came. I turned and started walking nervously out of the ballroom to lead them to the interview area where Alex Wallau was waiting. I led this pack of an entourage into the hall. It was maybe five hundred yards from the other ballroom where Alex was set up doing his interviews. Everyone is chattering when suddenly I hear Rory say, "Yo, Champ, this guy does a great YOU."

Everyone stopped walking except for me. I heard Tyson say, "Hey fat boy, is that true? You think you do a good ME?"

You know that feeling when you're driving on the highway and you're going along at a good clip, maybe twenty miles an hour over the speed limit, and you see what you think is a cop out of the corner of your eye? That feeling like you're having a heart attack? That was it. I felt like I was having a heart attack.

"You think you do a good me?" He repeated. "Let's hear it."

I was well and truly terrified. I began to stutter and try to explain, "No, no, I don't, it's not good, you won't think it's good, no I can't, I don't—"

He walked right up to me, still shining with sweat from his workout that would kill a Navy seal, with his face right up to mine,

"DO IT!" He demanded.

I took a deep breath and looked him right in the eye.

"Lisssssten you mutha fucka, you better get your sissssssy punk assss out of my faccccccce," I said, cramming in as many words with "S" in them to sell the bit, "Or I'm gonna drive your nossssse into your brain, then I'm gonna pisssss in your fuckin SSSSSSSSKULL, bitch!"

The guys in the entourage were shitting themselves—silent but frantically covering their faces and gyrating to hide their laughter. There was a long pause as Tyson stared into my face, head cocked sideways like someone looking for a book on a shelf. Finally, after what seemed like an eternity, he spoke.

"I don't have a lisssssssp, you fat fuck." He lisped.

Another long pause.

I felt like I was going to die right there on that spot.

Then he couldn't hold it anymore and broke out laughing. So did the guys. *Raucous, approving laughter.* He put me in a headlock under his sweaty armpit, tugged a few times, and then put his arm around me.

"That's a better ME than I do, you silly mother fucker," he said.

We proceeded to the ballroom and I felt like I was one of his entourage. I hung with them during the interview, and they invited me to hang out later as they were going to *hit some spots.*

Strangely for me, I did the sensible thing and declined. I had other ABC stuff to do that night. Yes, I could have hung with Mike Tyson and his peeps, but I didn't want to put my little ABC per diem job at risk. But it wasn't little to me, and I must have been doing it well, because they hired me back week after week, three more times to Atlantic City and once they even flew me to Vegas.

Barely two months in, July 13, 1989, I was hired to work on *Monday Night Baseball.* Wow. Yankee Stadium. Al Michaels, Tim McCarver and Jim Palmer. The Royals were in town and ABC was broadcasting the game because Bo Jackson had successfully made his return to baseball after hip surgery, even making the All-Star team. By now, I knew my way around, after all I'd been working for ABC for two whole months, and had my very own credential—the all-important all-access pass.

I arrived at Yankee Stadium, the cathedral of baseball. I'd never been there before. My first time there and I had ALL ACCESS. Amazing. I knew some of the crew from working boxing coverage. The producer was Curt Gowdy, Jr., son of the legendary announcer. Pre pre-game, my assignment was to shadow Al Michaels and do whatever he needed. He asked me to go down behind the home plate area and make sure they were set up for him to do an interview, then go to the Royals clubhouse to the training room and get Bo Jackson. I walked right into the Kansas City Royals clubhouse and straight to the training room where the most immense person I'd ever seen was on a table getting a rubdown.

Now I told you about Tyson. Bo Jackson made Tyson look like a mini-Bo. Carved out of granite, this guy was chiseled and GIGANTIC.

I spoke to the trainer. "I'm here to bring Mr. Jackson to his interview with Mr. Michaels."

From face down on the massage table, Bo looked up at me.

"Hey man," he said, "Be right witcha."

He grabbed a warm-up jacket, and in baseball spikes he walked with me across the cement floor under the stands to behind the home plate area where Al Michaels was waiting. We didn't talk on the walk over. We probably couldn't have heard anything anyway over the sound of Bo Jackson's metal cleats thundering with each step across the pavement. I brought him to Mr. Michaels and then it was off to my pre-game position. I had a few minutes so I went to a secluded area under the stadium and smoked PCP—otherwise known as angel dust.

Did I mention that by then I'd decided PCP was even better than cocaine? Well, it was cheaper anyway.

I had no fear of being caught. *So smart. So stupid.* I figured as long as I did my job impeccably, who would know?

Curt Gowdy Jr. gave out the pre-game and game-time assignments. Mine were simple. Pre-game, go to Bob Sheppard's legendary announce booth, introduce yourself to Mr. Sheppard and then cue him to announce the Yankee's to take the field. Game-time, in the booth with the announcers assisting the stage manager.

The first job was critical. If a game isn't being televised, the announcer knows it's time for the home team to take the field once someone sings the *Star Spangled Banner*. But when a game is televised, unless a big star is singing the anthem, the network utilizes that time for very expensive television spots. Capitalism at its finest right? Bury the anthem and play a commercial touting hot dogs, apple pie and Chevrolet, the Heartbeat of America. Take your hat off, put your hand over your heart, and salute a brand new Silverado. So unless the runner (me) cues him, Bob Sheppard has no way of knowing exactly when to begin announcing.

There I was, high on PCP, and on that particular day at Yankee Stadium, the elevators stopped working. I had to walk all way up the ramps from street level where the production trucks were, to the fifth

Sarge

level announcers' booth. Somewhere in between making my way to the booth, a producer asked me to go up to the Yankees offices and wait by the fax machine in the vice president of media relations, Arthur Richman's office, for a critical document that was being sent from ABC that was *critical* to the broadcast.

I made a beeline for the Yankee executive offices and barged right in using my ABC credential as a deflector shield. The offices were actually pretty much vacant, because almost everyone was at field level for the pre-game festivities. I waited by the fax machine for what seemed like forever. Whatever this *critical* fax was, I knew it was a big deal. I'd learned quickly at *Wide World of Sports* that everything in live television was a big deal. I waited and waited and waited...

But I had to go to the bathroom. Number Two. And it couldn't wait any longer.

I peeked around a couple of corners looking for an office with a bathroom. I found one and got there just in time. I sat down and closed the door. After the first rush of relief, I looked around and noticed that it was a pretty nice bathroom. But it had no fan and I didn't see any air freshener. The smelly evidence of my visit was going to be a source of considerable embarrassment if I couldn't vacate undetected. I was just about done when I heard someone moving around in the office outside the door. From a seated position, I cracked the door an inch. I could see George Steinbrenner at his desk picking up the phone.

I'm in George Steinbrenner's private bathroom. Kill me now. How am I going to get out of here? What if he wants to use the bathroom?

I peeked again and again, and finally I decided to just go for it. I flushed and waved my hands around to try and disperse the unpleasantness, but it was no use. It was a swampland. I walked out and it startled him.

"Who are you and what are you doing in my bathroom?!"

I flashed him my ABC credential. That seemed to solve the problem, but what he said next was legendary.

"Oh, well we love ABC, and my house is your house, but my shithouse is MY SHITHHOUSE! Now, carry on young man."

I got about five feet from his office door.

"Son, what did you EAT?!"

What did I EAT? Little did he know, I'd gotten high less than an hour ago under the stands. I went back to the fax machine and the fax was there. I tore it off and ran the ramps to the broadcast truck, sweating like a pig. I slammed the fax on the producer's desk and as I flew out the door to get up to the announce booth, I heard someone yell, "Better hurry!"

I went back in through the executive office doors, up the ramps, and directly to Mr. Sheppard's booth. I picked the headsets up off the floor to check in with the guys in the truck, and they were doing a check down of all cameramen and personnel to make sure everyone was online. When they got to me I heard, "Announce booth check?"

"Pickman in place, sir, ready to go," I said.

As the words came out of my mouth, Bob Sheppard craned around and asked me who I was and before I could answer, the bodyguard sitting next to him grabbed me while Sheppard was shouting, "Who is he?! Eject him from the stadium!"

Maybe if I weren't so sweaty, strung out, and high, I'd have been able to explain to Sheppard's satisfaction, but I'd neglected to do the one thing that is MANDATORY when privileged to be allowed in his announce booth. I had not properly introduced myself. I was too busy taking a dump in George Steinbrenner's private bathroom.

Suddenly I was being thrown out of Yankee Stadium, and I couldn't weasel my way out of it, no matter what I tried. The bodyguard dragged me down the ramps and used my shoulder like a battering ram to open an exit door out onto the Bronx streets. I quickly ran around to the executive office doors to make reentry but they were locked, and there was a security guy on the phone at the desk inside. I pounded on the door with my fist fast and hard. Another guard came but he wasn't letting me back in. I kept showing him my ABC credential and after much begging and fast talking he let me in, but the damage had been done. Apparently, when I did the headset check down with the truck, the ON key was left ON, and everyone wearing a headset up and down the line heard me being removed from the booth.

Worst of all in the eyes of producer Curt Gowdy, Jr., I had missed my game-time position, and the Yankees WERE NOT CUED by Bob Sheppard to take the field for several minutes while the announcers were left to speculate as to the lateness of their emergence. They were late because I fucked up and I'd be fired from ABC by Gowdy immediately after the telecast.

Did Sheppard overreact? Maybe. But none of it would have happened had I been on the ball and sober. *Thank you drug addiction.* An amazing opportunity down the drain, but it still didn't really register for me that my using was costing me so dearly.

Everything was someone else's fault.
The producer was an asshole.
The elevators were out. Probably because some asshole hadn't done his job to keep them running.
Bob Sheppard was an asshole for having me thrown out.

I was the asshole. But I wasn't about to admit it—to myself or to anyone else. I couldn't face the fact that I was a drug addict who couldn't get through a day without getting high. Drug use had cost me again, but I was undeterred.

As far as I was concerned, my firing was bullshit. I resolved to get another job immediately. I knew the name of an executive at CBS Sports who was the vice president of operations there, Arthur Harris, Jr. He was my next mountain to climb. I called the switchboard of CBS and asked for his extension and they connected me. The first time I called, I spoke to his assistant, Gina, and asked to speak with Mr. Harris. She politely asked if he could get back to me and I left my number. The next day I called again to find out if she'd misplaced my number because I hadn't heard from Mr. Harris yet. She was very polite.

"Mr. Harris does not know you and would like to know why you're calling."

"It's private and confidential," I said.

"Okay, I'll let him know."

I called Gina every day for a month.

"Please stop calling here. Mr. Harris doesn't know you and does not want to speak with you."

Could he have heard about me pooping in George Steinbrenner's office? Or the Mike Tyson episode? Or the Yankees not taking the field, costing ABC potentially thousands of dollars in dead air? *Naaaaah. No way.* He just doesn't *know* me, so he's reluctant to return my call.

To know me is to love me.

I decided to keep calling. It got to the point where I'd call the number, Gina would answer and I'd shoot the breeze with her.

"So, how's your day? It's your favorite call of the day."

Gina would laugh. One day, I didn't call and the next day when I did, she actually said, "I missed you yesterday."

"You did?"

"Yeah," she said, "I shouldn't be telling you this, but you're the only person who calls Arthur that isn't calling with a problem." Little did she know that I was heading for the homestretch of the biggest, worst problems of my life. That still didn't come across to most people—all they saw was my dogged persistence and unwillingness to take no for an answer. Ironically, these are two qualities necessary to succeed at sobriety, but I wouldn't call on those for a couple of years still.

One day I woke up late and was toying with the idea of NOT calling Mr. Harris that day, when lo and behold, the phone rang. It was Gina from Mr. Harris's office at CBS Sports.

"I've got Mr. Harris for you."

My heart started pounding wildly as I waited for him to come on the line.

"Mr. Pickman, Arthur Harris."

Not able to contain myself I excitedly blurted out, "Arthur!"

"It's Mr. Arthur Harris."

"Sorry, sorry," I sputtered, "Mr. Harris."

"I was in the shower this weekend and I couldn't get you out of my head," he began.

"You were in the shower and you were thinking of me? Really, sir?" Smartass. I just couldn't miss an opportunity for a dumb joke. I'm lucky he didn't hang up on me.

"That didn't come out right," he said. "What I meant was, I kept thinking about how you keep calling. You never give up, do you?"

"Well, no, not really," I said, "But I really, really want to work for CBS Sports."

"Why?"

"Sir, isn't it obvious? CBS has all the major coverages, MLB, NBA, NFL, Golf, NASCAR, Olympics? Come on sir, all due respect, but you guys need people working for you who never give up, no matter what, right?"

"Good point," he said. "However, I do not at the present time have a position available nor do I envision having a position in the near future." My heart started to sink. "But," he continued, "I would like to meet the most persistent individual I've ever come upon. Come to my office tomorrow morning at eleven."

"Yes, sir."

"If I let you come in, though, will you stop calling?"

"Yes sir, Mr. Harris, sir."

The next day, I put on my only suit and headed over to Black Rock, CBS Headquarters, on Sixth Avenue. I planned to make a strong enough impression that Mr. Harris would magically find a position for me where he claimed there wasn't one. I walked right into the building and straight to the elevators up to the twenty-eighth floor. I finally met Gina. She had been as big a part in me continuing to try and get her boss on the phone as I was, and I thanked her for getting me in. I was led into Mr. Arthur Harris, Jr.'s office and it was smaller than I would have imagined for a man of his rank and stature. He was a tall, large African-American man with a neatly trimmed goatee and glasses. He offered me a seat and his back was to the window.

"So this is what the most persistent man in the world looks like," he said. I thanked him. Then we talked about everything under the sun, and even though he made it clear that there was going to be NO JOB as a result of this meeting, he seemed to really like me. After about an hour of spirited conversation he asked me if he could take me to lunch.

"I'm gonna take you to my favorite place to get a sandwich in New York." We walked a couple of blocks up and one over to Seventh Avenue, and when we got to the corner, THERE IT WAS, the Carnegie Deli, my favorite deli on Earth. Some people are Katz's people, some are Second Avenue Deli people. I'm a Carnegie guy. The line, as always at lunch, was out the door and down the block all the way to the corner. Mr. Harris saw this and lamented, "C'mon, let's go somewhere else, I only have an hour."

I assured him we could go past the line and we'd be seated immediately. We walked ahead of the hungry hundreds, and Sandy Levine, the major domo of the greatest deli on earth, spotted me and shouted, "Bubbele! Come, come! How are you?"

I couldn't see Arthur's face, but I hoped he was impressed. Mr. Harris didn't know, but I'd been going into Carnegie since I was a small boy with my Poppy Herman, and I'd known Sandy since he took over after his father-in-law retired.

I was a *regular*—and fairly or not, I got preferential treatment. Here I was, jobless, but being treated like a conquering deli hero. We were seated at one of the long tables and enjoyed the quintessential deli lunch of a mile-high pastrami sandwich and Diet Dr. Brown's soda. We ate, we talked, ate, and talked some more. Then Arthur looked at his watch.

"I have to get back. Let's get the check."

But no check came. Mr. Harris summoned the waitress, and she came over.

"We need our check," he said.

"Sarge doesn't get a check."

Arthur looked at me in amazement.

"Who the hell are you?" he asked.

As we walked back to Black Rock and returned to his office, he kept reiterating that he didn't have a position for me. We sat down at his desk and he said it again.

"I really don't have a position for you. But if I did, would you be okay with not having an office or a desk?"

"No problem," I said.

"When can you start?"

"I already have."

He laughed. "Come in Monday and I'll figure out what to do with you."

Over the time I was at CBS Sports I worked on MLB, NBA, PGA, NASCAR, Boxing, Olympics, and even Pat O'Brien's brief but triumphant effort in late night, *Overtime*. I worked on *NFL Today*, a few Super Bowls, the World Series and NBA Championships.

I did well.

Arthur Harris, Jr. became a mentor to me in the same way George H. Barlett had when I was at Kent—a sort of father figure.

But I also continued to do drugs—my habit escalating—even as my bosses at CBS Sports gave me more responsibilities, and more than a few second chances.

One of the Last Straw moments for me with CBS Sports took place while high on PCP at the Spectrum in Philadelphia for Game Six of an NBA playoff series between the Sixers and Bulls. I was working the *Prudential At the Half* live from the CBS Broadcast Center in New York, a show hosted by Pat O'Brien and Bill Raftery. It was Mother's Day, so we had the mothers of NBA guys Bill Laimbeer, Isiah Thomas, James Worthy, and Michael Jordan in the studio for an appearance on the show. Afterward, I was dispatched to chauffeur Michael Jordan's parents to the Spectrum, seat them at the game, collect them at game's end, get video of the two of them together, and drive the tape to New York for use on the *CBS Evening News*.

I arrived at the Philadelphia arena with Moments to go in the third quarter, seated the Jordans, and then went back out to the car to get a joint of angel dust. I smoked it before going back into the arena. I woozily flashed my all-access credential to the guard as I re-entered, high as a kite. I made my way in the stadium down to press row and there was not one empty seat.

"Excuse me, pardon me, excuse me…"

I didn't have any official function at the game until it was time to drive Michael Jordan's parents back home, so it wasn't like I had a designated seat. I didn't care. I brashly made my way through the press area of the huge game, then through thousands of screaming fans, and I noticed a folded padded seat propped up against a side wall. I was so high, and so tired—all I wanted to do was sit down. I folded down the seat and nonchalantly sat. I was courtside and there were headphones on the ground next to the seat, so in order to look official, and since I was wearing a press credential around my neck anyway, I put on the headphones. There were usually left there for sideline producers to monitor reports by Jim Gray from courtside. Through the headphones, I could hear the producer and director barking commands to cameramen on one side and the announcer play by play in the other.

It was only then that I realized that I was seated at the far end of the Sixers' bench.

As I listened to the cacophony of voices in the headsets I heard Dick Stockton, the play-by-play announcer, in the right headphone say, "And as you look down the Sixers' bench, you can see Philadelphia's beleaguered big man Rick Mahorn with his foot in a bucket of ice. Wouldn't Billy Cunningham like to have him back in the game?"

In the other ear, I heard the producer Bob Mansbach screaming, "Camera Four, stay on the bench!"

He paused.

Then in a torrent, "Is that Pickman on the Sixers' bench!? What the fuck is Pickman doing on the Sixers' bench? Pickman is on the Sixers bench, and he's wearing cans (industry vernacular for headphones)! Camera Four, stay on Pickman, Pickman if you can hear me nod your head!"

I remember nodding and looking around trying to figure out which camera had me in its sights

He screamed, "What are you even doing here!? He's not on our team, Pickman what the fuck are you doing on the Sixers' bench, get the fuck out of the Spectrum, you're fired, you're fired!"

The producer had no idea I was legitimately at the game to deliver the Jordans and capture footage post-game of Michael Jordan with his mother. He thought I was there pulling some kind of stunt. He went crazy that I was at the game, crazy that I was on an NBA bench and he fired me from CBS Sports. Undeterred, I removed the headsets, fetched the Jordans post-game, shot my footage, drove the Jordans to the airport, still high on PCP, and returned to New York—videotape in hand of Michael hugging and kissing his mother after the Bulls' victory on Mother's Day.

Mission accomplished.

That was Sunday.

Monday, I just came to work like nothing happened.

It was four months later when I ran into that same producer at Flushing Meadows at the U.S. Open tennis championships. I was walking west and he was coming towards me from the east.

"Pickman, what are you doing here?" he asked.

"I'm working the Open." I was pretty sheepish, knowing that he would definitely remember firing me.

"Who are you working the Open for?"

"Ummmmm, us, CBS."

"US? CBS rehired you?"

"Well... no. I never actually left."

"I fired you! I fired you at the Spectrum in May!"

"I didn't think you meant it. So I kept coming to work."

"You didn't think I MEANT it!?" He was incredulous.

"Well," I stammered, "I knew you were busy and might not tell anyone that you fired me, so I kept coming to work."

He laughed. But it was an ugly laugh. He didn't think I was cute or funny, and he seemed disgusted by me disingenuous show of unmitigated gall. He made his position very clear.

"Stay away from the courts, stay away from the players, and stay away from me. I don't want to see your face or hear your voice for the two weeks that we're here, are we clear?"

We were clear.

Misunderstandings kept piling up. Sometimes whatever went wrong wasn't specifically my fault, but my behavior and attitude were so all over the place, that even when I was in the right, I found a way to make myself look entirely in the wrong. I was at CBS for about two more weeks until I was finally fired for good—over another *misunderstanding*.

I was a cat who had finally run out of lives.

Shortly after that, my use of angel dust and crack rendered me homeless. They say addicts must hit bottom to have even a chance of getting well. My bottom was coming up to bite me in the ass. At the time it felt like the end of the world—the lowest point of my adult life—hell, of my WHOLE life.

Now I've come to see it as the end of a nightmare.
And the start of the miraculous journey I've been on ever since.

HITTING BOTTOM

I never told anyone I was fired from my job at CBS Sports. I was too proud and too ashamed. *Isn't that funny—how pride and shame can be so closely linked.*

My drug use had escalated dramatically. I had a virtually unlimited expense account while working at CBS—so much of the job involved greasing various wheels with cash to make absolutely sure that nothing stood in the way of our live broadcasts. My two hundred dollar a day habit wasn't a problem financially as long as I could still make CBS pay the tab. But once the expense account was gone, I had to come up with that two hundred bucks every day somehow on my own.

So I lied and I stole.

Since no one knew CBS had fired me, I could use my pretend job to help make my lies believable. I had a scam going where I'd call people I knew, tell them that my CBS rental car had been towed with my wallet in the glove compartment and that I needed four hundred bucks to get the car out of impound. Everyone in New York City knew that getting a car out of impound was exorbitant, and no one questioned it. I even showed up at Greg Gumbel's apartment on 57th Street and pulled that move with him. It worked.

I reassured all of my *marks* that as soon as I recovered the vehicle, I'd go to an ATM and get them their money. But once they gave me the money, they never saw me again. I stole from everyone in my address book all over New York—friends of my parents, college buddies, former CBS co-workers, models I'd represented, and friends from childhood. My addiction robbed me of my integrity, robbed me of my dignity, and by extension, robbed anyone I could get in touch with who was kind enough to want to help me.

Having lost my sublet, and with an escalating appetite for street drugs, I found doorways and park benches to pass out on by night, and bars in dodgy parts of the lower east side to drink in by day, where I smoked my drugs in the bathroom. Occasionally, I'd turn up at my friend Todd's apartment at 30th and Park to hang out with him.

Todd and I had become friends back when I was in the model business and he was head of dress buying at Macy's. We were two straight men occupying jobs usually held by gay men. He was also an avid sports fan, and once I started working at CBS Sports, I got him hired to work in the studio on *College Football Saturdays* and *NFL Sundays* as a stringer in the background of studio shows. We had partied together, but our bonds were deeper than I suspected at the time.

Todd never suspected I was homeless.

I showered at my friend Russell's health club and laundered my only clothes at laundromats near welfare hotels. I'd show up at Todd's when I knew he'd be home, and many times he'd invite me to sleep in his loft.

He always hung the suit he wore from that day on the chair of the dinette, and in the breast pocket was his wallet. He'd turn in around eleven at night, and I'd pretend to go to sleep in the loft. I'd wait until he was asleep, then sneak down, boost his ATM card, go to the Citibank on the corner of 32nd and Park, and withdraw the maximum. I knew he never checked his bank balance because of the piles of unopened statements on the dining room table. Also, I knew his PIN because on one occasion he was late for a date, and asked me to go get him some cash from the corner.

His PIN was KIWI—the name of his cat.

Todd thought I was still working at CBS Sports, so anytime I needed some money and wanted to come in from the cold New York streets, I'd pop in on Todd and pull the same move. He'd be up at seven the next morning to shower. I'd pretend to have slept, even though I would have been up all night smoking drugs. On those mornings, I'd pretend to leave for work with Todd, and we'd share a cab to 34th Street, where I'd let him out, and he paid for the cab to take me uptown to CBS. Of course, I would just get out a block later, and, Todd's money in hand, I'd scamper over to Madison Square Garden to the escalators up from Penn Station and cop some *tall boy* vials of crack from the Dominican dealer working the morning rush crowd. Then I'd head back crosstown to Todd's place to smoke crack all day. Nude, alone, and catastrophically paranoid, I'd spend eight hours on his couch smoking crack.

I was ashamed.

But not ashamed enough to stop.

I did it several times a week. The rest of the time, I roamed the subways and the areas south of Houston Street, and the Manhattan Bridge. In order to keep the lie of my CBS work life going, I had to *disappear* for days at a time, so I could *reappear* and pull my scams on Todd.

I *reappeared* at Todd's one day, as he was leaving for work, and told him I had the day off. He offered to let me hang out at his place, and maybe we'd have dinner when he got home. Sure, dinner. I hadn't eaten anything really in what seemed like months, yet I wasn't really losing any weight—even though I only ate maybe every fourth day. My showing up at Todd's that day was actually convenient for him, since some movers were scheduled to come and replace his twelve-foot leather sofa. *Could I stay and wait for them? Of course.* Anything for Todd.

What happened is a story I tell often in recovery rooms around the country, from Los Angeles to Delray, Florida. It's part of my *story*— the journey I share about my journey through recovery, that hopefully can inspire addicts about how low I went, and how great my life is now.

People who've heard me speak even shout out to me sometimes. "Tell the Couch Story!" They request it—like a favorite song.

The Couch Story

While waiting for the men to come replace the couch, I descend madly into yet another crack binge. I'm nude on the couch when the buzzer rings.

The buzzer rings!

I freak out, thinking that the FBI—who I'm sure has been watching me from a window in the ad agency in the building across the way—is finally closing in on me.

The FBI often bursts in on obese nudists sitting on the couch in a cloud of crack smoke. Insane. But in my paranoid state, it was terrifyingly real.

I gather all the full vials of crack and swallow them, five or six in all. Crack stem in one hand and lighter in the other, I approach the ominous buzzer by the apartment door.

Crack addicts all relate to this, because for some strange reason, we will never put down either lighter or crack stem—holding them in a clenched death grip.

So I answer the buzzer in a whisper through clenched teeth.

"Yeeeeees?"

A sinister man with a heavy Israeli accent replies.

"It's Moishe's Movers, this is Avi, I'm here to get the old couch and deliver the new one."

Oh shit, I forgot, the couch movers. Oh my God, I ate all my crack!

If I could reach into myself and grab the drugs from my stomach, I would. I even think about taking a steak knife from the kitchen and cutting myself open to reclaim the drugs I think I need so desperately.

I would later move my bowels in a colander and sift through it to retain the vials which were covered in feces.

I buzz Avi up and continue freaking out, but I get it together enough to put on some briefs and wait for the doorbell to ring.

The doorbell rings.

I look through the peephole, still vaguely suspicious. But confident that this guy is not an FBI agent, I opened the door. To this day I remember the astonishment and disgust on this guy's face as he scans up and down my body.

"Wow," he says, "Wow. Okay. Where's the couch?"

Crack stem and lighter firmly still in my clutch, I lead him to the living room, and point to the huge sofa.

"Well, it's obvious this didn't come up in the elevator," he says. "We're gonna have to send this over the balcony and bring the new one up from the street the same way."

Then he makes a sour face and in his heavy accent says, "Mister, your breff stinks, why you don't brush your teef."

He leaves to get rope.

I do not brush my teeth.

He comes back and begins to harness the couch with movers' straps he ties together. He looks around and announces, "We need to tie this rope to something heavy that can turn, to anchor the rope. Come here, Fat Boy, I tie the rope around your waist and you go in the other room and close the door."

"Okay."

"You spin around and wind the rope around you, and when you hear me say TURN, you turn and let out some rope."

Simple.

I go in the other room and spin around and around

and around until I'm tied up like a damsel on a train track, still with crack stem and lighter in hand. From the other room I hear a muffled shout of, "TURN!"

I turn and let some rope out.

"TURN!"

He is lowering the couch from the balcony to his partners at street level, ten floors down. I do as I'm told, and it works. The couch safely reaches the street.

Now we have to bring the new sofa up.

Avi informs me we'll do it the same way but in reverse. I tie the straps around my waist and he heaves the other end from the balcony.

"When I yell 'OY' you TURN!"

I'm supposed to spool one revolution to take up the slack as we pull the new couch up over the balcony from the street. So I do it.

"OY!"

I spool.

"OY!"

I spool.

This goes on for fifty or sixty spooling moves. I'm all wound up—STILL with crack stem and lighter in hand. He's *oying* and I'm *spooling*. Then I hear something worryingly different from down below.

"OHHHHHHH SHIIIIIIIT!"

I start to unspool.

The couch is plummeting and I get dragged from the bedroom into the living room, hitting walls, bare feet sliding like I'm the Coyote in a Road Runner cartoon being dragged from behind a moving truck. I'm halfway across the living room and on my way to the balcony, tied to a couch which is making full use of gravity when Avi grabs me in a bear hug. We fall to the floor and are face to face right by the doorway out to the balcony and we abruptly stop.

Again, Avi says, "Oh, my GOD, your breff!!"

I was ashamed.

"You know, Fat Boy," he says, "If I don't catch you, you would have go over the balcony, and I'm pretty sure you don't land on couch."

Later that day, after the couch is safely installed, I go through Todd's drawers looking for anything of value that I can convert into cash for a day's worth of crack cocaine and bourbon. In his sock and underwear drawer I immediately hit pay dirt—two very expensive looking watches in felt bags, some rings, a bracelet, and some cufflinks—all gold, all pricey. Insane from my need to continue using, I grab the goods and hoof it over to the diamond district, where I go from jewelry dealer to jewelry dealer in an effort to sell Todd's heirlooms.

"My Grandpa left them to me," I tell the jewelers, and they believe me. I guess I don't look like a drug addict—I'm too FAT to be a crack addict—right?

Finally I settle on a jeweler I like. For Todd's Van Cleef & Arpels eighteen-karat gold watch I get two hundred dollars. It's worth over five thousand. For his Ebel peacock face gold watch I get a hundred and fifty. Pennies on the dollar. The guy in the yarmulke ends up giving me five hundred bucks for the whole booty—bracelets, cufflinks, gold chains, and watches. Twenty thousand dollars of jewelry sold for five hundred bucks by a fat crackhead, looking for two days of toxic gluttony—an orgy of PCP and Jack Daniels.

Literally a month goes by.

It's getting close to Christmas and I need cash to stay high. Todd is the only non-homeless person I still know, and as best as I can figure, he hasn't yet discovered that his priceless possessions are missing.

It's Christmas Eve, 1990. I show up at his loft duplex and he buzzes me up.

When I come in, he's looking for something—going in and out of the bedroom, opening and closing drawers.

"What are you looking for?" I ask. In all honesty, I was too strung out to imagine that he might be searching for the very things I had stolen.

"Could you help me?" he says, "I hid my watches and bracelet and ring from myself and I'm not sure where I put them. You take the living room and I'll keep searching in the bedroom."

He's shaking shoes and going through suit pockets.

"Sure."

I go out to the living room and start pulling couch cushions out and putting them back.

Then it hits me.

This is a great guy.

Todd is one of the most wonderful people you could ever meet, a real peach of a human being. Shame and regret overwhelm me.

I should not have robbed this man. It was deeply, morally, tragically WRONG.

"I took them!" I blurt out from the living room.

"What?"

"I TOOK ALL OF YOUR STUFF!"

"C'mon, buddy, stop goofing around. I'm going to Colorado skiing with my family, I wanna bring my watch and bracelet."

"I took your stuff and sold it in the jewelry district and that's it."

They say an addict will steal your stuff, but a dope fiend will steal your stuff and help you look for it. I was a dope fiend.

Todd comes into the living room and looks at me in disbelief.

"Why would you do that?"

"Because I'm a crack addict and I can't stop."

He looks me up and down, eying my girth.

"Aren't crack addicts like skinny and sickly?"

He can't bring himself to insult me by actually mentioning my weight. Even when confronted with a thief, a friend gone bad, someone he opened his home to who has robbed him, he doesn't insult me.

"Yeah, I'm fat." I say, "I'm a big fat crackhead and a thief."

He doesn't skip a beat.

"Then lets' get you some help.

With Todd's help, a day later I met with Vince Casolaro, an interventionist. A day after that I was on the steps of the Beachcomber Treatment Center in Delray Beach, Florida. A gigantic, bearded, soft-spoken man named Mike greeted me.

"Are you an alcohooooooolic?" He dragged out his words like they were coming out in slow motion.

I quickly fired back. "No, I'm a crack/PCP addict and I only drink when I can't get drugs, to take the 'edge' off."

"Riiiiiiiiiight." He stroked his beard. "How many drinks did you have on the plaaaaaaaane?"

I thought for a Moment, recounting them in my scrambled head.

"Eleven! I had eleven drinks on the plane."

"Oh goooooood," he said, "You're definitely NOT an alcoholic.

An alcoholic would have had "Tweeeeeeeelve."

Now who's the smartass?

"Okay," he says, "So here's what I want you to do. I want you to go in the other roooom and hit your kneeeees and praaay for the obsession to drink and druuuug to be removed from your liiiiife."

For some reason I complied.

I'm not really sure why, even after all this time.

For most of my twenty-nine years to that point, I'd been unhappy, insecure, obese, afraid, and NON-compliant—unwilling to listen or do what was asked of me. I would later learn that because I'd arrived at my bottom, *ready to take direction,* I had half a chance of beating my addiction.

I went in the other room and did what Mike told me to do.

I sat in a chair, and with my hands, palms downward, hit my knees over and over. I wasn't trying to be cute. Kneeling wasn't part of the Jewish tradition, so *hitting my knees* meant hitting them with my hands. I repeated the phrase, "Please, God, remove the obsession to drink and drug from my life. Please, God, remove the obsession to drink and drug from my life."

When I emerged from that room, having prayed to God, it didn't at first seem like anything had changed, but something had.

I never took another drink of alcohol or any kind of recreational or non-prescribed drug since.

One prayer changed my life.

The next morning I woke up at five thirty and began treatment. It must have been eleven in the morning before I realized that I hadn't thought about getting drunk or high. No detox. No detox meds. No hocus pocus—unless you think prayer is hocus pocus.

Figuring out the *hitting my knees* thing took another couple of weeks, when I was assigned a roommate named Rusty. That night before we turned in, Rusty knelt at his bedside in the prayer position.

"What are you doing?" I asked.

"Hitting my knees," he said. ""I'm hitting my knees then going to bed."

I paused, watching him, taking it all in. I too had been told to hit my knees, but for two weeks I'd been sitting on my bed and patting my knees with my hands, *hitting my knees* while I prayed for a better day. *Oh. THAT'S what they had meant.* I hadn't even been praying right, but for some reason it had worked anyway. I no longer had the desire or the inkling to drink or get high, even though I hadn't been able to stop for the better part of ten years.

I don't know why it happened for me like that, but I'm grateful it did. As I watch others grapple with addiction, and as I see some relapse, I thank God that I was freed so miraculously of my desire to drink and drug.

Yes, that moment was miraculous.

But in the years that have followed, I've worked diligently to keep that miracle alive, in myself, and hopefully, in others. Things changed for me in an instant—but my life remained transformed because of decades of commitment to working at it.

The fact remains, my prayers worked for me as nothing else had.

And Todd. *Where did he come from?* How did a human being so loving, forgiving, and compassionate cross my path. I've spent every day since I got sober trying to be more like him. At the most critical make-or-break moment of my life, he did for me what I could not do for myself—he got me to reach out and find the help I needed to get well.

This is the way most spiritual people describe destiny—a hidden power that guides what happens to us. Yet as I've learned from years of spiritual practice, the future is a collection of NOWS. That night, so many years ago, Todd was perfectly in the NOW, and I owe all good things in my life today, to a guy whose name just so happens to rhyme with GOD.

Go figure.

HALFWAY TO CONNECTICUT

Forty-two days of drug and alcohol treatment included countless hours of group and individual therapy, meditation, and straight talk sessions. It was made very clear to me that I had a sick ego. If I was ever to have a life without substance addiction, I'd have to be willing to take direction, listen, and have my ego crushed. As though the reality of the way I had been living wasn't enough, it was also made clear to me that I'd have to be open to confrontation about my behavior and attitude. I was also taught that this would be the first thing I'd ever finish.

Upon graduation from the Beachcomber, a next step was recommended. I was to live in a halfway house and attend ninety twelve-step meetings in ninety days—at least one per day.

An elderly man named Ron Martin picked me up from treatment and drove me to my new home in his Dodge Dart. The windows were barely cracked and he had a lit Pall Mall in his thin slit of a mouth.

Like my parents.

Ron didn't talk much, but he gave me one direction that has always stayed with me.

"Shut the fuck up and listen—that's half the battle."

Apparently, for me, the other half of the battle would be surviving the ride to the halfway house without getting lung cancer.

We arrived at NuWay Halfway House in Lantana, Florida, 503 West Pine Street, one block from the headquarters of the National Enquirer. This was where I was supposed to make good on my month and a half in treatment. I had no car, no possessions, and no idea what was going to happen in my life—but I was coached, trained, and convinced to believe that if I kept praying for each day to be better than the day before, it would.

A guy apparently in authority at NuWay named George told me one thing right up front. I had to get a job within twenty-four hours of this moment. *Or your shit will be by the curb.*

I knew they meant it. Some other guy's *shit* was at the curb when we pulled up to the property. Rent was one forty a week and I was expected to pay every Friday. *Okay, so now it's real.* I went to bed that night in a room with four other guys.

All of them knew the ropes.

All of them had more time sober than I did.

I hit my knees and went to bed.

I woke up the next morning at a quarter to five, not realizing it would be my routine wake-up time. Sleeping felt good. It had been six years since I had really experienced sleeping through the night. I got dressed and went into the kitchen to look for a cup of coffee, and a guy was already up having a bowl of cereal. He said he was going to the gym. I asked him if I could come along.

"Sure."

We went to his gym, Fitness Today. It was about five miles from the house. It was twenty minutes after five in the morning, there were about a dozen people standing outside the gym waiting to get in, looking like a bunch of methadone addicts or Black Friday shoppers. Five minutes later, an amazingly buff guy arrived and opened up the gym. I followed him into his office.

"Can I speak with you?" I asked.

"How can I help you?"

"Are you doing any hiring?"

He looked at me. "Are you up every day at this time?"

"Yes."

Honesty is a very important thing in recovery. I told myself I was being honest—maybe I'd only gotten up one day at this time, but if you've only been in a place for one day, than that one day qualifies as being EVERY day. Or something like that…

"Great," he said, "I'm Dave. And you're my new opening guy. Here are your keys."

He hired me on the spot, like a fix was in or something. He toured me around, told me what I'd need to know to open the club, and presto! I was employed. Amazing.

Every day, I got up at four and walked the five miles from NuWay to Fitness Today. In the absolute darkness, I trudged my fat ass to work every day. I was so thoroughly grateful. And I didn't even mind the early hour—I'd been getting up every day in treatment at five thirty to do a power walk before breakfast.

It became my routine. I'd go to work early, and every night, I'd hit a recovery meeting. I could always get a ride to a meeting with one of the guys at the house. We were actually encouraged to ask for rides home from men at the meeting. It was annoying at first, having to rely on other people, but that was actually the whole point. We needed to learn to rely on each other as sober men.

If we learned how to ask for rides, it would teach us how to ask for help when we needed it.

One person I knew I wanted to ask for help, was a man named Jere Henderson, who had come to speak to our group when I was in treatment. I knew I wanted him to sponsor me—to take me through the twelve steps and act as a mentor and guide as I made my way forward through recovery.

I ran into Jere all the time at meetings, and every time I asked, "Would you be my sponsor?"

He always blew me off. "I'll see you next time."

Until, one Sunday morning, when he finally decided to say yes.

"I think you're willing now," he said. "I think we can work together. Call me every day at ten to six in the morning."

And I did.

Every day like clockwork I called him from work. We only talked for fifteen minutes or so, but I really looked forward to those conversations—mainly because of what he would say at the end of every call.

"I love you."

"I love you too," I'd say.

So simple. But something I'd never really said or heard with any real regularity in my life. It was easier for me to hear it than to say it, but from those daily conversations, I learned to say "I love you."

Jere taught me everything I know and would need to know.

Here's a partial list of some of the wisdom and spiritual philosophy Jere shared with me which I refer to every day and pass on to the people I have the privilege of working with on the journey of recovery:

> Other people's feelings are none of my business.
>
> The voice in my head is the voice of my ego, it always speaks first, it always speaks the loudest, and it's always, always wrong.
>
> When someone compliments you just say "Thank you, that's a nice compliment."
>
> In all painful chapters of your life, pray for the lesson to present itself.
>
> Worry about nothing. Pray about everything.
>
> Forgiveness offers me all that I want and the sooner I forgive myself the sooner I will be able to experience joy
>
> Love is all there is and serving the universe is my job.
>
> My career is maintaining my sobriety and passing it on to others. Everything else is icing on the cake.
>
> Even if I let go of some thing or situation, it can't be taken away if I don't release it too.

Jere was a real character, who had been married five times, had done time in prison, had robbed banks, was a highly sought-after baseball pitcher who chucked baseball so he could drink, drug, and commit all kinds of mayhem, and he once had avoided a prison sentence by serving in the Navy.

Who said being sober was boring?

Jere got sober late in life. Stories of his crack addiction, his toupee, his three-wheel moped and Nazi helmet, and his job as a grocery store bag boy at age fifty are still the stuff of South Florida sober legend. I was fortunate to have had as much time with Jere while he was alive, and he was the perfect sponsor for me.

He always reminded me that things could get better and better in sobriety, and very, very gradually, they did.

I knew I couldn't keep walking to work forever, but didn't have a solution. One morning at the gym, my boss remarked on the fact that he had noticed I was sweaty every day first thing in the morning. We both knew I was overweight, but my shirt was absolutely soaked with sweat. I shared with him that I walked to work. He was shocked to learn I had to leave my residence an hour and fifteen minutes early every day to make it to work on time. The next day he showed up with a used ten speed bike with a derailleur that was rusted in tenth gear. It was a dream come true. Now, I could sleep an extra hour and leave the house at five in the morning to arrive on time.

I was so grateful.

A few months later I saved a couple of bucks and with a birthday check from my folks, I purchased a used Yamaha Riva scooter with the governor removed. A Sherriff's Deputy's kid had owned it and had altered it so it went sixty-five miles an hour.

Now I could leave the house just five minutes before I needed to be at work. Another half-hour of sleep! Life was improving incrementally. A dollar filled the tank on that scooter right up to the gas cap, but every dollar counted. I was barely making minimum wage at Fitness Today, and I groused to Jere about it. He said if I wanted a better situation that I should pray for it, do the footwork, and things would improve. I did exactly what Jere said to do and several days on my lunch break from Fitness Today, I rode around the area looking for a new job.

One day, I wandered into a new store called Home Depot. That was before they took over the planet. I had done the praying, so I

Sarge

figured *doing the footwork* required that I walk in and fill out an application. Then let my higher power do the rest. As I passed through the doorway a man was at a makeshift podium in the doorway greeting customers. He was a thick bodied man with huge glasses and a deep resonant voice.

"Welcome to Home Depot, young man, I'm Norman."

"Hey, nice pipes," I said.

"Those are in plumbing supplies," he said, "Aisle Eight."

"No, sir," I said, "Your voice. I mean your voice. Nice pipes."

"Thank you!" he boomed.

"Are you hiring?" I asked. "I'm looking for a job, sir."

"You and everyone else in South Florida."

He opened a drawer in the podium and showed me what seemed like a thousand submitted job applications stuffed inside. But he gave me a blank application anyway.

"Here," he said. "Fill this out and bring it back."

So I did, and brought it back to him.

"That was quick," he said. "Where are you from?"

"New York City," I said. "I'm living in a halfway house in Lantana and working as a janitor at a health club."

"I'm from New York too," he said. "Westchester, the suburbs."

"I know it well," I offered.

"Well," he said, "We're not hiring, but let me check on something, and I'll be right back."

I waited. A moment later he returned.

"If we had a spot for you, when could you start?"

Jere had told me that if anyone asked me when I could start, my answer should be, "I already have. I'm here, aren't I?"

So that's what I said to Norman. He laughed—his laugh was like baritone music—and he told me to come in on Monday dressed for hard work

"I'll wear my welding helmet," I said.

He laughed again. I loved his laugh. More importantly, I had just been given another gift, I thought.

I thanked my boss at the health club and showed up for work the next Monday at Home Depot and found Norman. He took me out to the parking lot and told me that I was the new *lot guy*—it was my job to bring the carts in from the lot and patrol for trash. I was the happiest guy in the world. Not only was I scooting to work in seconds flat on my jet scooter, but I didn't have to be there until eight o'clock!

Can someone say UPGRADE?

There was only one problem. After taxes the money wasn't much better. Every two weeks I netted two hundred ninety eight dollars. My rent at the halfway house came to two eighty. That left me eighteen bucks to make it through two weeks.

Jere told me to pray for help.

"Remember," he would say, "Worry about nothing, pray about everything."

I prayed my ASS OFF. Somehow, I survived. Plus, it wouldn't have killed me to eat less, given I was over three hundred pounds and riding a powder blue scooter. People told me it looked like there was no scooter and the wheels were coming directly out of my ass.

Norman Stillman invited me to his home for meals prepared by his wife Helen, and I swam in their pool. He befriended me. It turned out I was the ONLY person from work he'd ever had over to his home. He took me under his wing, and taught me the ropes at Home Depot. It was a special relationship.

After three months, I was promoted from bringing carts in from the lot to a position as a cashier. Again, irony. I was a retired drug addict and thief, being coached and sponsored by Jere, a man who did time for robbing banks, and here I was, handling thousands of dollars a day.

Another irony: Eventually an imbalance with my cash drawer got me fired. But it wasn't missing money. It had too much! I came out over a few times—I don't know how—and company policy was that after a certain number of times with the cash in your drawer not balancing, you were out. It made no sense to me, by that time, Norman had been promoted to district manager of a dozen Home Depots.

Again, Jere came up with a great idea.

"You play the piano don't you?" he said. "Why don't you get a job playing the piano?"

I was skeptical. "How am I gonna do that?"

"Drive around on that scooter of yours," he said, "And walk into every place that looks like it might have a piano. Just sit down and start playing it."

I got on my scooter and started driving around. I walked into a couple of places in Boynton Beach and was asked to please leave. I figured I'd work my way down to Boca Raton.

After trying a few places and being asked to please not play the piano, I happened into a place right in the heart of Delray on the Intracoastal Waterway next to a bridge. It was an Italian bistro/restaurant and I forget the name, but I walked in and there was a gorgeous white piano.

No one was around, so I sat down and started playing.

A gentleman came out of the kitchen, and he stood and listened.

"Can I help you?" he finally asked.

"I'm looking for a job playing the piano," I said.

"Can you play some Sinatra?"

You want Sinatra? I can give you Sinatra.

I played Sinatra song after Sinatra song and he seemed to enjoy it.

"When can you start?" he asked.

I thought of Jere, and said, "Haven't I already?"

"Great," he said, "You have no idea how good your timing is. The guy who was here before— he was one of those alcoholic guys in that *program* and he musta started drinking again 'cause he hasn't shown up all week."

I wasn't going to tell him that I was also one of those alcoholic guys, but that I was sober. Some info is on a need-to-know basis. I wasn't using, and I needed the job.

"How much do you get?" he asked. Then he answered his own question and said "I can only pay you one thirty five a night plus tips."

"I get one forty," I said. I wasn't trying to play hardball—in my mind I was thinking per week, not per *night*!

"Okay, one forty, five nights a week. You start at seven and end at eleven. You get dinner before or after your show. See you tonight."

Is there a God? You tell me.

I was making one forty a week for forty hours of work, and now, doing something I'd been doing since I was five, which I LOVED to do, I'd be getting seven hundred bucks a week

PLUS TIPS!

For twenty hours work. I was ecstatic. I went over to Jere's apartment, which coincidentally, ridiculously, was only one hundred yards from the new job. I could not have been more over the moon.

As a matter of fact, I just remembered the name of the restaurant— Luna Ristorante. The Moon.

I was there for months and saved around three grand in no time. I sat down at seven and took no breaks.

Jim, the owner, kept imploring me to take a break.

"Musicians take breaks!"

"Are you kidding me," I'd say, "I'm so grateful to be here, I'm not getting up from this piano until you shut off the lights and lock the doors."

But one night, I came in, and Jim met me at the door with bad news, that he didn't need me anymore. The guy I'd replaced, the alcoholic, was sober again and had come back—and the thing was— the guy was dating Jim's sister, so Jim's hands were tied.

He had to take the guy back.

I was crushed. I'd been making great money, but BOOM. Gravy

train OVER. I called Jere.

"DO THE FOOTWORK! Worry about nothing, pray about everything."

Hmmmmm. I still had my homemade sportscasting demo tape. I decided to resurrect my dream of being a baseball play-by-play announcer. I read in the paper that the Major League Baseball winter meetings were being held in Miami at the Fontainebleau Hotel. So I came up with an idea. I'd make up a couple hundred cassettes of my demo tape and I'd go down to Miami on my scooter and hand out tapes in the lobby of the Fontainebleau to anyone and everyone.

I went to Sam's Club and bought a gross of disposable take-out boxes, bought a bunch of peanuts in the shell, put a little spork snack-pack in the box, along with my demo tape, and made up stickers to put on the outside.

Sarge—the Play-by-Play Guy TO-GO with.

Good idea right?

I spent the next two days making up the boxes.

A friend with a car dropped me off at the Fontainebleau Hotel. I schlepped a hundred and fifty of those packages filled with peanuts inside in two huge trash bags. I found a bellhop and gave him fifty bucks and asked him to get me one of their cool, swanky bellhop carts. I loaded up the cart and stood in the lobby handing out *Sarge—the Play-by-Play Guy TO-GO with* boxes.

I decided I wouldn't leave until I handed them all out. I got there at nine in the morning and sometime around ten that night I only had one left. I could swear, I'd talked to everyone in that hotel. Even the bellhops and concierge had my demo tapes.

I took the train home to Boynton Beach. By the time I got home, my roommate told me that the phone had been ringing all day.

I had five appointments I had to call back about immediately to meet with baseball people about play-by-play jobs!

I made the calls. They were all minor league general managers.

Hey, I'll take it.

Wichita, Kansas.
Sarasota, Florida.
Abilene, Texas.
Salt Lake City, Utah.
Bend, Oregon.

I rode my little scooter to Miami Beach the next day for my appointments.

The Texas guy was my first meeting. I met him in the coffee shop at the hotel.

"You're Sarge?" The guy from Abilene asked.

"That's me," I said.

"Oh, yeah, sorry, we were lookin' for a totally White fella. Thanks for comin' down."

Is it easier when the racism is unapologetic? I don't know.

I had the other meetings, but it turned out everyone was meeting with dozens of other applicants as well. My last interview was with the guy from Bend, Oregon. *The Bend Rockies.*

We dispatched with the pleasantries.

"I want the job." I said.

"Well," he said, "You know, it's awful White up by us."

"That's okay," I said, "I'm from New York. I grew up around snow, I can handle it."

"No," he said, "I mean the folks are White."

Thanks for clearing that up.

"But," he went on, "I guess they could get used to you. The pay is only eight fifty an hour, but you can travel on the team bus and eat with the players."

Eight fifty an hour?!

"No thank you," I said. "I was making more at Home Depot bringing the carts in off the lot."

"We got a Home Depot about sixty miles from us!" he said, "And

I know the manager!" As if that was an amazing way to make the situation work.

"I'm gonna have to decline," I said, "But thank you."

Back to the drawing board.

But this time it would give way to me finding my profession. I was reading the paper while I was on the Stairmaster at the gym and saw a classified ad for a bar in Boca Raton that was looking for *Comedians and self-contained variety acts for Monday's Open-Mike Night*. Haggerty's in Boca was the place, but there was only one problem. The show started at nine and my curfew at the halfway house was ten. Plus, Haggerty's was a bar, and the LAST PLACE an addict in recovery should be hanging out is a BAR.

I went to the halfway house office and asked permission to enter myself into the contest and permission to overshoot curfew. George told me as long as I bring someone with over five years of sobriety with me, I could enter the contest—as long as the contest was the only reason I was going to a bar.

"I've wanted to be a comedian my whole life. Maybe this is my chance?"

That was good enough for him. I asked a guy named Timmy with more than five years of sobriety who I'd met at one of the men's recovery meetings to accompany me to the comedy open-mike night, and off we went. There were dozens of hopeful comedians there and I signed up. The only material I had was impressions of Mike Tyson and Marv Albert but they were dead on, so that was the material I'd go to open-mike war with. Once I signed the clipboard at the bar to perform, there was no turning back, but my insides began to liquefy. I hustled to the men's room in the back and just made it, but I remembered something Jere told me. "Worry about nothing, pray about everything." So I closed the toilet lid and hit my knees and prayed to get through this and for my higher power, whom I choose to call God, to give me the courage to make sure I didn't let fear keep me from trying stand-up. It's a ritual I've subsequently repeated thousands of times in men's rooms all over the world, and I've always gotten through my performances.

I came out and couldn't wait to go on.

But I was low on the list so Timmy and I would have to wait until all of the other clowns tried their shit on the sparse crowd. Finally, it was my turn. The emcee took the mike.

"Our next contestant hails from New York City," he said, "Give it up for SAAAAAAAAARGE!"

I bounded up on the stage. I really don't remember what I did, but I do remember hearing Timmy laugh at everything I said. I finished with a flourish doing an impression of Marv Albert on the toilet announcing a game between the Chicago Bulls and the Jackson 5. The small audience roared with laughter and I was done.

Bitten hard by the comedy bug.

I loved it. People in the audience were laughing at stuff that I'd been doing for years—but only to my friends. Now I was on a stage, entertaining for real, and it gave me a feeling of total accomplishment like I'd never experienced. It was more than working through my fear and performing in a contest—I was HOME and it was amazing. Two more guys performed and then they invited all of the contestants on stage for the judging. We lined up and the emcee held his hand over each comedian's head. It was all about audience response. A real scientific approach. He went from guy to gal to guy and there was some cheering. Then he put his hand over my head and the crowd of forty or so people went crazy.

I won.

Do you want even more ridiculous irony?

The prize was fifty bucks worth of drink coupons for the bar. Timmy, my sober companion looked at me with a grin.

"You're not planning on keepin' those are ya?"

I handed him my free drink coupons and he gave them to one of the other comics. I went back there eleven straight weeks and won every time. Every week I gave the drink tickets to another performer, unlucky for not winning, but lucky for getting the free drinks.

And the die was cast.

I was certain beyond a shadow of a doubt—in a way I'd never felt before—of my future. *Comedy*. I figured if I wasn't supposed to pursue stand-up comedy, than the universe wouldn't have seen fit for me to win. For me, it was spiritual proof that I was pretty good.

Once I reached eight months sober, I moved into my friend Timmy's sober house which was managed by none other than the human chimney, Ron Martin, who had picked me up from treatment in his Dodge Dart the day I graduated.

A sober house has fewer restrictions than a halfway house, and I was able to go out on my own and perform at as many open-mikes as I could find. I drove that scooter all over South Florida from Jupiter all the way to Coral Gables, risking my life every night on I-95, buzzing along in the right lane going sixty-five miles per hour on a sewing machine on wheels.

That year I also was lucky enough to fall in love with a girl named Liz. Like a mini-Madonna, she rocked my world. All the guys wanted her, but one night, I got up the courage to ask, and she was willing. We went off riding my scooter on a date, she became mine. I met her in the recovery community and I learned from that relationship, that I could have fun sober. There was companionship, and sex, and laughter. She was awesome. She was sober too, and young and gorgeous and talented in her own right. She could see someone in an outfit she liked, go to the craft store, buy fabric and make the outfit. The relationship didn't last long, but the love she showed me, and the friendship we shared, was emblematic of what I found in the new community of recovery where I was finding myself.

Before Liz, I'd never had a real girlfriend before. Relating to someone with both of us clean and sober makes all the difference in the world. It was the same with the friends I was making. The connections were, deep, real, and they lasted.

There I was, though, doing stand-up, and I had a hot chick, plus I got a little gray cat I named Furillo, after Daniel J. Travanti's *Hill Street Blues* character. I had money in the bank, I was killing 'em at the open-mike joints, and I wanted to get back to New York somehow, some way. I read in the *Sun Sentinel* that a summer camp was looking for a head counselor and the owner was interviewing potential candidates in Key Biscayne at the Hilton.

I called Lou Weinberg, who's incidentally the brother of Springsteen's drummer Max Weinberg of *Conan O'Brien* fame, and made an appointment. I drove the scooter down to Key Biscayne from Boynton Beach, a seventy-nine mile jaunt. I met with Lou and all I remember is that he hired me and I was headed to camp in the Pocono's.

Pocono Highlands Camp in Pennsylvania.

Not so different from the Catskills. And a lot closer to New York than Florida was.

I said my goodbyes to Liz and everyone else and headed to summer camp.

I had several days before I needed to go to camp so before heading for Pennsylvania, I went home to visit with the folks in Long Island. We shared information about our lives very selectively. It would be a long time before they knew much about my exploits in the preceding ten years. While I was there, I heard that ESPN in Bristol, Connecticut, was looking for production assistants.

I called George Veras, an Emmy award-winning producer for CBS Sports and a true mentor. George had called and written me while I was in treatment and was so loving and supportive. There were many times that those notes helped me believe I could get through it and find my way back to being something in the world. When I was a low level assistant to the producer at CBS, George let me go out with a crew on several occasions and shoot and edit my own stories for *CBS Sports Saturday*. A couple of them even aired on the broadcast during boxing coverage. He was a husband, and a father and a great boss, a real mensch.

I told George I was back from Florida and that I had fifteen months sober. I thanked him for the kind letters and calls while I was getting my shit together, and I told him I heard that ESPN was looking for guys. As my last boss of record, would he mind calling there and helping me get an interview.

"Colleague," he said—that's what he called people on the phone, in a deep, resonant voice. "Colleague, it would be my pleasure."

The next day I got a call from ESPN to come to Bristol and meet with a guy named Al Jaffee. I don't remember much about the interview, just that they were seeing two hundred twenty-five applicants and Jaffee told me to not hold out too much hope. But he did decide to test me a little.

"Who were the pitchers in the bullpen for the Chicago White Sox last year?" he asked.

"Easy," I said. "Shawn Hillegas, Bobby Thigpen, Melido Perez, Ken Patterson, Greg Hibbard, and a very young Alex Fernandez."

You could have scraped Al Jaffee's face off the floor.

"Wow," he said, "No one's gotten that one."

"What else would you like to know?" I asked quietly. Maybe it was all that prayer and sobriety, but I wasn't showing off. He asked a question, and I answered it. I just wanted to know if he needed anything else from me.

"No," he said, "I think I've got what I need."

I thought it had gone well, but I didn't expect anything. I went to Pennsylvania and showed up at the Pocono Highlands Camp. I was head counselor with an entire bunk to myself—*Oh, the luxury!*—and I was in charge of the senior boys' side of camp. I had the best time of my life with those kids. I loved them, and I think, for the most part, they loved me too. I made them write home every other day, hoping to make their PARENTS love me too, since visiting day is when the gratuities usually flow. I was sailing through the season. Three days before visiting day, an announcement came over the camp loudspeaker.

Sarge, please come to Lou's office.

Wonderful, I thought, three days before visiting day and I'm getting fired. Through my ten-year odyssey of hiring and firing, I'd come to view every call to someone's office as bad news. I found Lou and asked what was up.

"Call your mother," he said, "Immediately. It's urgent."

My mind began to race. *Did my father die? What?*

I used Lou's phone and called my Mom.

"ESPN called," she said. "They want you to come work in Bristol."

"Now? But visiting day is in three days and I stand to make a killing in tips." *Talk about not seeing the bigger picture.*

"Tips?" she asked. "What are you going on about?"

"Okay," I said, "I'll be home tomorrow to pack some things."

Tomorrow. God. *Where will I live in Bristol? What's the pay? OMG. ESPN?* I told Lou I was leaving, and he didn't seem too broken up about it. I duffle-bagged my stuff, and then realized, what about my boys? I called an emergency meeting and got all of my boys together, about one hundred fifty kids. I told them I was leaving. I got very emotional. That's what experiencing life sober can do, allow you to feel how much things matter—and these kids mattered to me—well beyond the potential tips from their parents. I was tearing up as I told them that I was going to work for ESPN, but that I loved each and every one of them as if they were my own, and that without me there, maybe they'd have more chances to sneak out of their bunks and go over to girls' side now. That got a cheer.

I went home to get ready for a new amazing chapter in my life. I put my dreams of being a comedian to the side for the time being—*I mean, come on, it's ESPN!* Maybe someday soon I'd be an anchor on *Sportscenter*. Thank you God.

ESPN in 1991 was not the ESPN we know today, but it was an exhilarating, phenomenal exercise in dedication and precision the likes of which I'd never known. *ABC Wide World of Sports* and CBS Sports were great, but ESPN was a place where the ONLY thing that mattered was sports—it didn't have to compete with entertainment shows or news.

Living in Bristol, Connecticut notwithstanding, I loved my time at ESPN and developed a mentor in a wonderful, loving, passionate human being named Barry Sacks. He remains my pal today. Bristol on the other hand was a town of a couple of big box stores and a Dunkin Donuts drive-thru.

We worked seven days a week, many times for ten-hour shifts, watching games, then writing and editing together highlight packages for *Sportscenter* and the other studio shows in the broadcast center. The pay wasn't bad for 1991—ten bucks an hour for the first forty hours, and double time for every hour after that. I loved it there. I got to work with now world-famous talent and hand in my work to them on a daily basis.

I loved working for Keith Olbermann—one of the strangest, but most amazingly talented guys ever. He was quick with a kind word, complimentary when you presented him with a well-produced package, and he would come and find you in the bullpen to thank you for your work.

Robin Roberts treated me with such respect and goodwill—one of the most down-to-earth, lovely, and wonderful people you'd ever want to work for. Many Sunday mornings I'd arrive at seven for the ten o'clock Sunday morning *Sportscenter* she anchored alone, and Robin would bring me coffee and a bagel and we'd work together on getting the scripts ready, making each other laugh the whole time.

"Get down with your baaaaaad self!" she'd tell me.

Chris Berman—Famous for being *Boomer* and for giving people nicknames. He had a comfortable, bold style, and he gave me not one, but two nicknames, a fact I remain very proud of to this day.

Dr. Strangelove and *Slim Pickens* (a play on Pickman).

Actually, Slim Pickens was also an actor in the movie *Dr. Strangelove*, hence BOTH nicknames came from the same movie. One amazing thing about Chris is that he remembers EVERYTHING. Once, in 1998, nearly six years after I'd left ESPN, I was at the baggage claim at the Cleveland Airport—I was there as a comedy act for the Major League Baseball All-Star game. Looking for my suitcase, I heard a man's voice booming from four carousels over.

"Slim Pickens! Moving up in the world, performing with the Beach Boys for the *All-Star Game*! Awesome! Just Awesome!"

Then he added—and this blew my mind—"How's Donna Summer treatin' ya?"

How did he know that I was touring at the time as Donna Summer's opening act?

He came over and gave me two passes to a cigar party being hosted on the Flats in Cleveland—a special event hard to get a ticket to. He made me feel like a million bucks.

Chris Myers and I worked the early morning two o'clock *Sportscenter* shift with Linda Cohn, another peach of a human. Chris was funny and liked to laugh, on the air or off. We traded barbs companywide at one thirty in the morning over the network-wide public address system. He was another phenomenal *Ted Baxter*-esque talent with a huge heart and a warm presence. We'd be on-air partners for a brief time on the inaugural season of FOX Sports Radio and it was Chris that made that happen for me. He tragically lost one of his sons last year in a brutal car accident and my heart hurts for him.

Tim Kiely produced the same hour of *Sportscenter* with Chris and Linda and we had a ball together. Tim is presently the Emmy Award-winning producer of TNT's studio show with Barkley and Kenny

Smith. I should give him a call and yank his chain one of these days.

Howie Schwab, Jack Edwards, Mike Tirico, and many, many others at ESPN treated me with respect, spoke to me like I was a friend, and made the entire experience phenomenal.

Unfortunately I was a couple of years ahead of my time. I had a style to my highlight packages. I would try whenever possible to infuse comedy in my scripts for the talent and in my highlights. Frequently, I'd be cited by the executive producer and upbraided.

"THIS IS SPORTS NEWS, NOT COMEDIC ENTERTAINMENT!"

When it was time for my six month review, I was asked pointedly by the eight producers seated around the conference room table where I saw myself in five years.

I told the truth.

"I see myself anchoring *Sportscenter*."

WRONG ANSWER.

They were looking for someone who wanted to PRODUCE *Sportscenter*—not become the on-air talent.

Barry Sacks, my guy, took me aside.

"I tried to enlighten them," he said, "But I was outvoted. You have five more weeks, so finish strong."

They'd just cut me loose and I'm supposed to stay for five more weeks?

But I took Barry's advice, finished strong, and that was that. When it came time to leave I called my old buddy from CBS Sports, Ted Gangi and asked him what he thought I should do now.

After all I'd been fired from three major networks at this point and maybe the handwriting was on the wall for me.

"You're the funniest guy I know," Ted said, "Why don't you be a comedian in New York. Come, stay on my pullout couch, and go for that."

"Really dude," I said, "You'd help me do that?"

"Yeaaaaaaaaaahhhh," he said.

I loaded my Honda Civic wagon and pointed it towards 8th and

Bleecker in Manhattan, one hundred seven miles down the road. It turned out to be the greatest and most prophetic move of my life.

MY MAN SAM

A great sportscaster named Sal Marchiano, who worked at ESPN in Bristol, Connecticut, and then had a twenty-five year career in New York City on WNBC, once famously quipped, "Happiness is Bristol in your rear view mirror."

I wasn't happy to have been invited to clean out my locker by the powers that be at ESPN, but, it would turn out to be one of those life defining moments that shape the rest of your life.

I moved to my buddy Ted's rent controlled apartment in the West Village. Another great thing about Ted's place was that there was a recovery meeting place right around the corner on Perry Street that had a six thirty morning meeting. I was two years sober and I knew that the key to the rest of my life was to go to meetings, stay sober, have a higher power, and let everything fall into place.

Jere taught me that, and I believed.

Bristol was in my rear view mirror and the rest of my life was in front of me. I started below the bottom of the stand-up comedy ladder as it were. I showed up at every open-mike night in New York, usually with Ted in tow. The whole point is to get stage time, and after all, I did have some jokes I wrote in Florida, a damn good Mike Tyson— and don't forget my Marv Albert was the best in the business. Armed with literally nothing to say, I showed up at every restaurant from Morningside Heights to Sheepshead Bay in search of an open-mike night that would give me a shot.

One night, while hanging around a restaurant with a microphone in midtown, I met Sam Brown. Neither of us got to go on that night, but we struck up a friendship and from that night forward, Ted was off the hook. Sam and I quickly became inseparable—sure that the universe had introduced us for a reason. We were both aspiring comedians in New York, and for two difficult, frustrating, exhausting, income-less years, it was Sam and Sarge, Sarge and Sam. We weren't a comedy team but we definitely were a team. Every day we'd get together, either Ted's apartment on Bleecker and 8th Street, or at his place on the Upper West Side, and we would try to help each other come up with a comedy act. Before meeting Sam, I had enrolled in a comedy class called Manhattan Punchline, but Sam and I could accomplish in two hours what I couldn't even begin to do in two months taking this particular class. (The class was taught by Lee Frank, a successful comedian and writer, and a wonderful guy as it turns out, but there was something special about the connection between me and Sam that made things click in my mind.)

Sam and I would write for each other and try out the routines. We'd "sell" jokes to each other, a process where one guy would come up with an idea and try to prove to the other guy why we thought it was funny. Then we'd embark on the journey of signing ourselves up for the "open-mike nights" of New York, always held at venues not known for presenting "real" comedians. Hamburger Harry's backroom, the West End Gate Bar and Grill up by Columbia University, the basement of a Mexican place in the Flatiron District, the Eagle Tavern, the Duplex (a gay sing-a-long club with a 55 seat room upstairs aptly named "Upstairs at the Duplex"), Don't Tell Mama, Rose's Turn, and Cha Cha's—later the venue of my FIRST PAID GIG!

When we couldn't make it on stage at any of the dozens of open-mikes, we'd go to the YMCA on 66th and Broadway, down the block from ABC Television, and take turns performing for each other all afternoon in their *theater* room. I'd sit in a chair in the middle of the room and Sam would get on stage, then we'd switch. We DID grow a lot, but in the beginning we were awful. I mean horrific. But we pushed one another to get up there. We were neurotic and mortified. However, we were driven. Driven to DO THIS. We helped each other get past the butterflies in our stomachs—not just butterflies, PTERODACTYLS. This more than cemented our huge love for one another. I'm not entirely sure what our partnership meant to him, but for me, I can honestly say that if it were not for Sam and his faith in my talent, I would not have continued my aggressive pursuit of a comedy career—with its endless opportunities for total humiliation.

I trusted Sam's judgment implicitly and totally respected his opinion. He was genius level—intuitive and articulate, passionate and crazy. And we both had mothers we KNEW were nuts. Sam was also rich. He lived on the inheritance left to him by his father who passed when he was twelve. But he was the kind of rich guy who knew how lucky he was to have what he had, and he was generous—helping so many people on the street unobtrusively, because he felt a kinship with *the crazy ones* and related to them in a way not many did. Maybe feeling crazy is true of a lot of creative people, but the loss of his father fueled his angst. He was a seething cauldron of creativity and desire to express his pain through a filter of darkness and imagination. It had a depth I'd never seen before and haven't seen since.

We were scared and desperate and determined, and in love with the idea of becoming comedians... BECAUSE WE HAD NO CHOICE. We'd both demonstrated that we couldn't work conventional jobs. All we were hoping for was a comedy club that would let us be comedians. One showroom—ONE!—where there'd be people to perform for. In those days we didn't think of performing comedy to make people happy *per se*. We wanted our own lives to be validated. For both of us, it was the performing of a RANT that began in our gut—the dissatisfaction and immense mental anguish from being completely misunderstood by our respective families. We derived pleasure from the catharsis of bashing our families, unedited, as payback for every minute of living the torture of our lives with them. Through this process, we learned that stand-up comedy REQUIRES, absolutely insists that you NOT MINCE WORDS. Choose them carefully, but NO MINCING. Sam taught me how to dig and dig and dig to the depths of my true self, and find the stories and expressions to describe what felt like tragedy to me. Then you share those war stories, like soldiers coming home from war in one piece but in a million pieces all the same. Sam and I were stand-up comedy war buddies.

We became regulars all over town. I won a stand-up contest at the Duplex, where I got to relive my big win at Haggerty's in Boca. The prize included a write-up in *Backstage*, an industry bible. Winning gave me the ability to show up whenever I wanted and be guaranteed stage time. There were open-mikes and bringer shows, where if you bring five or six people to come pay for drinks, the place will let you perform. You run out of those six people pretty quickly when you're begging on at these places every night.

Winning also gave me the confidence to hang at other clubs around Greenwich Village, like Boston Comedy Club and the Comedy Cellar. The uptown clubs like Catch a Rising Star, the Comic Strip, and the Improv were as yet out of reach.

Getting up at the crack of dawn and living on triple espressos and going out every night until the wee hours can be a grind but Sam and I were both exhilarated. There were hours and hours of waiting around, but on most nights, not all, we could get on by just persevering. Many nights at the better venues you'd get there early and wait and wait and wait and just when it was about to be your turn, Sarah Silverman or Jay Mohr would show up and do an hour and kill like nobody's business and the night was over. You had waited for five hours but didn't get on, but we hung tough.

If you wanted any chance of getting work you had to have a tape.

A VHS tape. *Yes, it was that long ago.*

Andy Engel used to hold his *New Talent Showcase* at Caroline's on Broadway. Andy was an awesome guy and a terrific comic in his own right, but he must have loved being in control of other comics. If you brought ten people in, he'd put you on, and a guy named Pete Klusman would tape you on the same stage where they shot *Caroline's Comedy Hour* for A&E. Pete miked the crowd for great laughter audio and shot it like you were on a television show. If you had a good set, you could send the tape out and maybe get some work. I did his *Showcase* a half dozen times, to the point that Andy didn't even make me bring people anymore. I could actually show up at Caroline's on Tuesday night and do a REAL set in a REAL club.

Around then I met Roger Paul, a small time booking agent—kind of a *Broadway Danny Rose* type—but he got me work. If you had a car to get to gigs, and if you called in to Roger's office every day, and didn't fuck up, Roger got you booked. Today, he's a gigantic corporate entertainment agent in New York, but in those days, Roger found gigs for all the greats: Suzy Essman, Lewis Black, Jon Stewart, Jay Mohr, Dave Chappelle. You name a gig, Roger booked it. The only way you can get better at being a stand-up comedian is to WORK. Roger made that a reality.

I drove all over the eastern seaboard and around the south doing gigs that Roger got me. You start as an emcee making shit money and then you middle or feature, making… shit money. The ultimate dream though was actually getting paid to be a comedian. I prayed just to be paid to do stand-up.

One Sunday night, we heard about an open-mike at a place called Cha-Cha's in Little Italy. Lou "Baccala" Cary was hosting. Sam and I signed up and one by one, the comedians got up and did five minutes of their best material. They held the show outside, behind Cha-Cha's, and there were about sixty people seated on wrought iron chairs at tables, having desserts and cappuccinos. Next to the stage there was a statue of a woman holding an urn that had water coming out of it.

A stage next to a fountain. *Classy.*

From the stage you could see a collection of men in warm-up suits and loafers—*made men*—sitting in an oblong oval talking. I don't really want to divulge who exactly was at the table, because I love my life, and it's only pertinent in so much as they were *men* talking about *things*.

My turn came, and I blew the place apart with energy.

Sarge

When I first started stand-up I might have been one of the loudest comedians in New York. I was terrified, so I performed fast and loud. These days it's a fallback position, like shifting gears, but in those days I'd just blast away. I finished my set and I came off the stage and a big guy gestures me over.

"*Johnny the Cheetah* wants to talk to you," he says.

Gulp. "*Johnny the Cheetah?*"

"Yeah, the *Cheetah*," he says. "He wants to talk, he's in the back."

I went to the back of the restaurant and there was a half open door. I knocked. A guy with a dark black pony tail with a shock of gray hair from front to back was sitting at a desk, wearing Porsche glasses which were already twenty years out of style, and he was swirling a lowball in his left hand.

"Sit."

I sat.

"You're pretty funny," he said. "Where'd you get all that energy?"

"Thank you sir," I said, "It's the way I perform."

"I like it, I like it," he said, "Listen, I wanna book you for Sunday nights. You available Sunday nights?"

"Well…" I said, "I gotta move some things around, but yes."

I had nothing to move around. I would still wait four hours to watch other comedians get stage time, while club managers would shove me out of the way to find REAL comics.

"You come down seven sharp on Sunday nights," he continued. "I'll give you twenty-five bucks and a dessert and a moccacino."

I shook his hand.

"I'll be here. How much time do you need me to do?"

"An ow-ah," he said. That's Brooklyn for an hour.

"An hour? I only have ten minutes of material."

"That's okay, you'll do it six times."

"Six times?"

"Yeah, six times. Next week, seven, don't be late. Ciao."

I walked out of that office ten feet off the ground. Twenty-five dollars AND a dessert, AND a moccacino. MY BIG BREAK!

The following week I showed up at a quarter to seven for my dessert and my moccacino. Lou Caray wasn't there, and there weren't any other comics. A crowd was gathering in the back outside for the show and the same oval of men in warm-ups from the week before. *The Cheetah* gets up on stage and introduces me.

"He just got back from Vegas, he plays Atlantic City, clubs all over New York, put your hands together for Serge."

I wasn't going to correct him. I spent all week worried about these ten minutes. I tried to write some more material but when I got on stage all that would come out was the ten that I had been doing for the last month or so—a couple jokes, the Mike Tyson impression, the Marv Albert impression—then I'd start over. Some people were laughing, some weren't listening—especially the guys in the oval, half of them had their backs to me. I got through it six times. They told me to get my money at the counter at the front and I could go. I came back every week for about seven weeks in a row. My act began to grow to the point where I only had to repeat it five times instead of six to fill the hour.

One Tuesday I called in to Roger to check in.

"I got a gig for you in Virginia. Roanoke, Virginia," he says, "Four hundred fifty dollars. One show Thursday night, two shows Friday, two Saturday and one on Sunday."

I'm there. I called everybody I knew and I was walking on air for the rest of the week, getting ready to leave for Virginia on Wednesday. I drove the ten hours to Roanoke, and stayed at the filthiest house I'd ever step foot in. Trash was everywhere, the sink was full of dishes, the beds were unmade AND I LOVED IT because I was on the road like a REAL comedian. I made radio morning show appearances, worked out at a local gym during the day and did shows at night. I was in paradise. At the end of the run, I got paid, and I drove back late

Sunday night, arriving home late in the afternoon on Monday. The phone machine was blinking the number thirty-two. *Thirty-two messages?!* I didn't even know the numbers went up that high. I pushed the button.

"It's six fifty and you're not here yet. BEEEEEP."

"It's six fifty four. Where are you, you Fat Fuck? BEEEEEP."

"It's seven. You better be walking in the door. BEEEEEP."

Holy shit! I'd forgotten about Cha Cha's!

"It's seven oh three. You're dead. BEEEEEP."

The rest were hang-ups and BEEEEEP.

Uh oh.

I sat down on my pullout bed and thought about what I was going to do. I sat there for about three minutes. The phone rang.

"Hello...?"

The voice on the other end didn't even talk to me. I could hear him saying to someone else, "He just picked up." Then to me, "Hold on, I've got the *Cheetah*."

My heart was in my throat.

"Come down to the club," *Cheetah* said. "And you better have cancer."

Now I was really scared. I headed out the door and went over to Cha Cha's. I nervously walked in and an elderly woman sitting next to the cheesecake carousel just pointed with her index finger towards the back. I went to the back and the *Cheetah* was on the phone.

I stood in the doorway.

"Yeah, listen," he said to whomever he was talking to, "I gotta go, I gotta take care of something."

Was he going to shoot me? Was there someone behind the door who would strangle me with a wire like in the movies?

My mind was racing as he slammed down the phone.

"SIT!"

I sat.

"Where the fuck were you Sunday?"

I couldn't even get words out of my mouth. It was kind like when Jackie Gleason on the *Honeymooners* would pace around behind Alice and stammer and stutter, mouthing words but no sound would come out.

"Virginia," I finally managed to say, "I wwwwwwas in Vvvvvvvirginia."

"VIRGINIA?!" He screamed, getting up from his chair, "VIRGINIA?! VIRGINIA?!" He opened the window behind his desk from the top pane and yelled out into the alley, "Virginia! He was in Virginia!"

Who was he talking to? Were there snipers? Was I in target range?

I mustered up the courage to explain.

"I got a call," I mumbled, "To go do some shows in Virginia."

He came down from the chair.

"How much did those scumbags pay to hire you away from me?"

He was livid. The guy was paying me twenty-five bucks and a Sfogliatelle for crying out loud. Then he went in his pocket and started throwing money on the desk in front of me.

"You want more money?! Is that it?! Money?! Because I can give you more money?" He continued, throwing more money on the desk. "You're booked here on Sundays, you Fat Fuck. I don't give a shit what you do Monday through Saturday as long as your Fat Ass is here on Sunday at seven sharp!"

"I'm sorry, sir," I said, "It will never happen again."

"I know it won't happen again," he said, "Because if it does, you told your last joke in fucking Virginia. Now GO!"

The following Sunday I came back, and for maybe three more Sundays after that. I only had to repeat the set three or four times by then, because I was actually developing more material. He gave me a raise to fifty bucks.

Then one Sunday, I headed over at six to go do my Sunday night lifetime gig, and the place is… GONE. I walked half a block towards Canal Street, then back past where Cha Cha's used to be. It was a burned-out smoldering empty lot, with yellow POLICE LINE DO NOT CROSS tape across it. Cha Cha's was no more. I had no idea what had happened, but I literally wept tears of joy. The gig was over. I was off the hook. I thought I was going to have to work there forever for fear I'd get rubbed out or something.

Three years later I finally got the skinny on what was going on at Cha Cha's. I was on stage at Caesar's Atlantic City opening for the Pointer Sisters or the Four Tops, I don't remember which, and I noticed Geno, a childhood friend of mine, in the front row with a blonde under each arm. His lion's head ring with the diamond in the mouth was blinding me as I walked around the stage. While I'm performing, I wondered if my friend Geno knew it was me. See, we grew up together on Long Island and I knew he was kind of a *connected guy*—if you know what I mean. After my set, I was in my dressing room and he arrived.

"Saaaaaaaaarge, you're Sarge!"

"Yeah, Gene, can you believe it?" I said, "I'm a comedian." "*You're Sarge!*" he says again, laughing, "Did you used to do a gig at Cha Cha's on Mulberry?"

"Yeah…?"

"Do you realize what that was?" he asked. "When they had you do the same material over and over and over?"

I stopped. "Do you know what the hell that was all about?"

"They booked you because you were the loudest guy they ever heard," he says, laughing harder, "And they could have their weekly meeting without the FBI hearing anything, even though they were listening in from a van parked down the block. You were the joke they played on the FBI! Nobody could hear anyone else because of YOUR BIG MOUTH!"

You could have knocked me over with a feather. My first paid gig was a joke the mob was playing on the feds. You can't make this shit up.

But as pleased as I was to have finished my run at the now pile of ashes formerly known as Cha Cha's, it still left me without a job. The idea that I could actually be a comedian and actually make a living doing it was at the core of all of my waking thoughts. Every tiny little indication inspired me, drove me, and helped me to not give up, no matter what. All it took to keep me going was a compliment about a performance from another comedian, or a club giving me a spot on a Tuesday night at six forty-five, or another comedian calling me to be on a show that he or she was putting together. Whatever it was, my mindset was positive because I was sober.

One day I was reading the *New York Post* and there was a Page Six blurb about Alan King picking the comedians for the first *New York Comedy Festival* and that Alan himself would be looking at up-and-coming comics in the back room of Carnegie Deli—*from five to nine in the morning*—picking ten to perform for the festival.

Maybe I had an edge.

Growing up in Great Neck, Long Island, everyone was aware that Alan King lived there. He was my idol. I'd seen him on with *Johnny Carson* my whole life. I'd seen him on *Ed Sullivan*. I even saw him in the Catskills at Grossinger's Resort and my Poppy knew him from the Friars Club. When I was a kid, on Sunday mornings, I'd wait outside the bagel store for Mr. King's Rolls Royce to pull up and he'd get out in his pajamas to go in and get bagels. When he came out, he gave me his change a bunch of times. So needless to say, I was in show biz love.

I took the train out to Great Neck and brought my demo tape from Caroline's to Alan's house in an exclusive part of Kings Point called Kenilworth. Kings Point was exclusive enough, but Alan lived in an exclusive subdivision within the exclusive subdivision. I rode my bike over to his house and knocked on the door. A Latina answered the door and I asked her to please make sure Mr. King got this tape as soon as possible. In the manila envelope, I wrote a note which told him of how he was friendly with my Poppy from the Friar's and how he used to give me his change in front of the bagel store.

That was my edge.

The night before Alan was doing his Carnegie auditions, I did four sets around town and then at one in the morning I went directly from the comedy clubs to the back door of the deli to wait on line overnight to one of the first ones Alan saw that morning. When I got there, two other comedians were already ahead of me. Thank God it wasn't that cold out, and we waited overnight for five to come. The line was forming quickly and ultimately by three thirty it was around the corner and all the way down the block, and around the other block.

At five sharp, the loading doors opened with a creak, and the first three acts were invited in. There was coffee and I had a cup. Sandy Levine, my old Carnegie friend came over.

"Sarge! What are you doing here?"

Before I could answer him I heard Alan King.

"Let's go, we got a lot of comics to see."

He was the great one, sitting at a four top, with a cigar in one hand and a glass of seltzer in the other, and a plate of prune danish in front of him.

Seltzer, a prune danish, and a cigar—staples of Jewish culture.

There was a small riser set up in front of Alan.

"Good Morning," he said, "Now, you're Sarge?"

"Yes, I am."

He pointed the cigar at me and shouted, "Go ahead! You're on!"

I was struck by a lightning bolt of fear so I just started with the Black Jewish jokes.

"I'm a Black Jew, I shoplift but just wholesale."

"All of my relatives were slaves. Sure the blacks were slaves, not funny, but it must have been hilarious when the Jews were slaves in Egypt. Hey Murray, help me move this pyramid."

Alan howled with laughter, however I thought he was being compassionate.

"Stop, stop, you're good, you've got it."

I've got it? I did three jokes. I hadn't even done a bit yet and I have it?

I nervously bounded off the stage and stuck my hand out and shook Alan's. I thanked him profusely again and again for the opportunity.

"Don't worry," he said. "I'll call."

I figured he was being nice. I hadn't performed enough for him to have seen anything. I walked out of the deli thinking he was being nice as he would be to all the comics. I semi-proudly walked past all the other, most of whom I knew, and they were full of questions.

"Is he really there?"

"What did he say?"

"Did you get it?"

I didn't know. Later that day, I got a call. Alan King booked me for ALL of the shows of the *New York Comedy Festival*. He looked at ALL of those hundreds of New York comics, searching for just ten, and HE PICKED ME.

Several weeks later, backstage at one of the big shows of the festival, Alan came back to tell everyone to break a leg. I asked him if I could talk to him for a second.

"It's the Black Jew, what do you want Sammy Davis?"

"I just wanted to thank you on behalf of my grandfather for watching the tape and helping my career by putting me in this festival. I am so grateful and I will not let you down."

He looked at me like I was crazy.

"What tape, who's your grandfather?"

"I'm from Great Neck," I said, "And I went out to your house and dropped off a package with a demo tape and a note."

"I didn't get any tape," he said, "I haven't been home to Great Neck in over a month. You're here because I think you're hilarious."

I still thought he was just being nice. He saw my hesitation, pointed at me, and winked.

"Just be funny."

So I was.

I prayed away the fear every night on my knees in the men's room before my shows. I didn't have the luxury of a couple of belts or a few tokes on a joint—I was operating on raw spiritual nerve and no matter what happened I trusted the universe to take me wherever I was supposed to go in this journey.

The journey took a huge tick upward one night when I decided to do Andy Engel's *New Talent Showcase* again at Caroline's. I was itching to make something, anything happen. I felt I was ready, and I invited all of the big comedy agents from places like ICM and William Morris to Caroline's on Broadway to come see the *Black Jew* blow the place apart. I don't know what possessed me. Andy gave me the closing spot. I prayed in the bathroom like always, and that night I had what I thought was the best set I'd ever had. I felt like I absolutely kicked butt. But in the immediate afterglow, as I wandered the club as it was emptying, I got a lot of compliments—but no action from any people calling themselves agents.

Well, I thought, at least I was taping, and it was a good set, so I'd have the demo.

The next morning around eleven I got a call.

"Sarge? Please hold for Conan Smith from William Morris."

Music to my ears. Conan had a handful of amazing, talented comedians under his representation including Artie Lange, Gilbert Gottfried, and many others. My heart began to race. *OMG, William Morris was calling me?!* Conan came to the phone.

"Sarge! Hello! Are you available to come up to the agency and meet everyone?"

"Were you there last night?" I asked.

"No," he said, "I couldn't make it. BUT I HEARD ABOUT IT! And that's even better."

The next day I was up at William Morris off Sixth Avenue, meeting with the team that would turn out to be my new agents.

It was definitely a game changer.

A dream.

After meeting Conan and everyone, he told me that they wanted to sign me across the board—meaning in every area of representation possible—television, film, voice-over, commercial and literary.

Booooooooooyah!

Conan was the nicest, coolest, most down-to-earth guy. I felt vindicated, and on my way to the top. We'd speak daily and once the gigs started materializing, the way I felt about my life and my chances were forever bolstered. One morning Conan called and told me I was booked as Natalie Cole's opening act. I needed to get myself to Cape Cod to a venue called the Melody Tent. I had no idea what to expect because until that point I'd performed at open-mikes, comedy clubs around the east coast, and a couple of private parties, but I was ready.

I mean... Natalie Cole!

I went to Cape Cod and showed up five hours early. I wanted to take it all in. I had a process for eradicating fear in those days. I journaled. I had read a book called *The Artists Way* and it recommended journaling as a way to dump your negative thoughts so they didn't stay in your consciousness and taint your artistic voice. I sat in the empty arena—a theater-in-the-round set-up—an island stage surrounded by more seats than I'd ever played to in my life. I sat alone in the third row and put pen to paper, feverishly trying to dump my fear.

I was terrified.

Then after about five pages of dumping I did what's called an *I AM* page. You write *I AM* at the top left hand corner and find as many positive words as you can to write about yourself.

I AM, resourceful, creative, improvisational, sober, down to earth, loving, kind, compassionate, human, dedicated, lucky, funny, competent...

You get the idea.

After the dumping journal and the *I AM* page, the fear eased. Musicians started to show up to the orchestra pit, and they began tuning their instruments. I introduced myself to everyone as Natalie's opening act and they were all cool. I was excited to meet her and retreated back to my dressing room to do my pre-show prayers. There was a knock on the door and a voice.

"Ten minutes, Sarge."

My insides were rumbling but I was excited—NOT scared.

"PLACES EVERYBODY."

A guy with a walky-talky escorted me to the arena about ten yards from the dressing rooms and positioned me at the top of a long sloping runway down to the round stage surrounded by Natalie Cole fans. The place was packed, not an empty seat. I don't know exactly how many people were there, but it looked like thousands. There was a fleeting second of doubt that flashed before through my mind. *What if I freeze? What do I say first? What should I open with? What if they hate me? OMG.OMG.OMG.* Then I got down to business.

"Good evening everyone and welcome to the Melody Tent for what will be a great night of music, but first let me entertain you for a few minutes while Ms. Cole gets ready to blow this place apart. I'm Sarge and I'm a Black Jew. That's right I hire myself to clean my own house every Thursday."

I got my first big laugh and I was off to the races. I walked around and spun around and whirled around playing all sides of the circular crowd, doing double set-ups of jokes and delivering punch lines with precision. The audience was eating it up and I was killing. In what seemed like seconds, my twenty-five minutes was done. It was time for the real star to come out. I wanted it to go on forever but I knew my place. I thanked the audience and told them Ms. Cole, who I'd still not even met, couldn't wait to come out and sing to them. I don't know where the words came from, the poise, the schmaltz, but I was a pro. I could do this. The second I made the long walk up the runway, through the crowd to the top of the venue, there she was, next to the sound mixing board booth, in a full length sequined gown. Physically statuesque and beautiful. It took my breath away. Natalie Cole was about to go on and she might have actually seen the last minute of my set. As I approached to make way, she gave me a thumbs up and winked at me.

"Great job," she said.

Natalie Cole acknowledged me!?

I was higher than on any drug. I just devoured my first challenge of performing for more people than I'd ever performed for, in the round, opening for a STAR. Her approval sent me into the stratosphere. I didn't go back to the dressing room. I stayed right next to the sound guy and watched the entire show. After that, I was booked to open for many, many stars, and I always watched the show from the sound booth. Partially because I was in awe, partially because I was too high from the experience to be alone, and totally because I was so damn proud of myself for even being able to do this.

The next day, Conan told me that I'd been hired for ten more Natalie dates. These paid between a thousand and fifteen hundred dollars per show. I was in show biz. All those open-mikes and hell gigs where I drove fourteen hours to Canada, Mississippi, or wherever had paid off.

Fast forward:

I moved to Los Angeles in 1995. Shortly after, Sam Brown, also moved to the Coast. I met my first wife, and my life began to change. Sam was still single—married only to comedy. We had no falling out, our lives just started taking different courses. I was opening for some of the biggest names in adult contemporary music, Natalie Cole, Donna Summer, the Beach Boys, Aretha Franklin, and Paul Anka, to name just a few. Mine was deemed a "friendlier" comedy voice than Sam's—he was darker, more difficult for some audiences to accept.

We continued drifting apart.

Fast forward again:

By 2012, I was living in Florida. I made one of my trips to Los Angeles for potential business. To save money I usually stayed at my friend's house, ridiculously, and ironically, my friend is also named Sam. Sam Bernstein. *You want more cosmic coincidence? Sam's husband is Ron Shore, a Jewish kid I went to Episcopal boys' school with in 1973.* I was parallel parking in front of Sam and Ron's house on Norwich Drive in West Hollywood, a block from Cedars-Sinai Hospital, which was clearly visible through the windshield.

My phone rang.

It was an old buddy of mine from the New York circuit, a brilliant comedienne, Cory Kahaney. She started in stand-up at the same time as Sam Brown and I. She was calling to tell me that Sam was gravely ill, and she knew we were close, and was sure I knew, but wanted to tell me how sorry she was for my trouble. I confessed to her how ashamed I was that I actually did not know about Sam being ill. We had not been as close as we once were, and had lost touch. She knew us when we were "Sam and Sarge." She knew us together and the way we were together and her first instinct when she learned of the seriousness of his illness was, *I have to call Sarge*. She and I also had not been in touch for some time. As I heard her say the words *pancreatic cancer*, I interrupted her.

"Where is he?" I asked.

"Cedars-Sinai in LA," she said, and my heart stopped. I could see the Star of David that adorns the top of that very hospital from where I was standing. I restarted the car and told her I was on my way.

I was cold. Numb. Embarrassed that this young man, who I loved so much, who I'd allowed myself to fall out of touch with, was—in Cory's words—*probably not going to make it.*

I raced down the one block to hospital parking. I got out of my car, and my feet didn't even seem to be touching the ground, and with an urgency I'd never felt before, I walked as quickly as my legs would take me to the elevators in the oncology wing where he was recovering from surgery. The elevator stopped on every floor, which only added to the angst. I stopped at the nurse's station and asked for Sam's room. The nurse pointed to the right. I nervously walked up to his room. Just seeing his name written on the sign outside the room made me sick to my stomach. The door was ajar, and I snuck in.

There he was.

Tubes, hoses, machines, flowers, and chocolates were everywhere.

Sam's brother, Adam, was there, his sister, Lisa, and there in the bed, SAM—ashen and gaunt, with those gigantic, crazy, beautiful eyes. We hadn't seen each other in over a decade. He looked at me manically, and with his right index finger, stretching the tube that was attached to his wrist almost to its limit, he said, "Sarge, don't you fucking dare speak."

"Why?" I asked nervously.

He winced. "Because it hurts to laugh." He turned to his sister, Lisa, and said, "Sarge makes me laugh harder than anyone else I've ever known."

With everything he was dealing with in that hospital room, he gave ME a compliment—the greatest compliment a comedian can give to another comedian. Then he did it again.

"Don't speak. If you speak I'll laugh and my stitches will come out."

They'd removed the cancerous part of his pancreas and he was optimistic. *My friend Cory was pessimistic. Was there something she didn't know? Was there something SAM didn't know?* Whatever his chances, I really did think that if there was anyone that would beat this thing, it would be my man Sam. Things had been going his way. He'd finally found love—the real thing—on J-Date no-less, and he and his wife had just celebrated the birth of their second boy. God didn't need him yet. But his family did. I did. We all did.

Was it denial or blind faith? I left his room that day believing wholeheartedly that he would beat the cancer. For each of the next three days I came back. He gave me permission to speak and even crack a few jokes. We got to be alone and I caught him up on my life. He wanted to hear about every gig, my family, my travels, all of it—and every time I'd start a story, about anything, he'd laugh. He'd been my best friend and comedy partner, and as I sat there at his bedside, I realized we were each other's biggest fans. We sat together and shared that laughter, amidst the rumpled sheets and the din of the medical machines that surrounded him.

My heart was crushed for him. The rest of my visits were not as private because other friends and family were there. People who'd become close to him since we grew apart, family, his gorgeous wife Ilona, his business partners, his agents. Suddenly I felt like I was in the way. I'd missed so much of his recent life. The other people around HIM deserved to be there. Did I? He got up several times to walk laps around the halls with his IV cart trailing alongside. I was honored to go on one of those walks. We hugged and I kissed him on the forehead.

"I'll see you soon," I said, "In this life or the next."

"Oh, I'm not done yet," he said.

Sam was so brave and so gracious. He was surrounded with love and that helped me to forgive myself for the time that passed. I wept in the elevator on the way down and then some more in the car. I couldn't get myself to turn the key. I called Cory back and told her about my reunion with Sam. We cried.

"I saw him Cory," I said between tears, "HE WILL BEAT THIS."

I couldn't even fathom the alternative.

Less than sixty days later he was gone.

In his life, Sam was relentless. He had guts, a scathing wit, an unquenchable need for attention, and a powerful desire to make something of himself. He didn't win this battle, but in fighting it, he gave me an even bigger SHOVE than he had always given me when we were inseparable stand-up comedy warriors. A shove to ponder my own mortality. A shove to love my life even more than I already did. An opportunity to love him in person one more time which gave me that much more gratitude for my own life. Most importantly, a shove to get on with doing the things in my life that need to be done because like him I could be gone in the blink of an eye, and what would my boy know of me? His passing has made me love my wife even more than I already do—my son, my comedy, my sobriety—my whole life and every moment in that life.

HOORAY FOR HOLLYWOOD

I had started working with Conan Smith at William Morris, and was opening for big stars. Meanwhile, a husband and wife team of managers from Australia, David and Christine Martin, had also signed me, though I was at the very bottom of their roster, under comedians like Louie CK—but I was just happy they liked me.

One night I was on my way to a comedy club on lower Broadway and I got a beep on my pager. It was a Los Angeles number I didn't recognize. I stopped at a pay phone.

"Hello, William Morris Los Angeles."

Oh! William Morris LOS ANGELES!

"I received a page from extension two-oh-four?"

"Hold on sir, I'll connect you to Jenny Delaney."

JENNY DELANEY! *Who's Jenny Delaney?*

"Hello Sarge, Jenny Delaney, head of tee-vee here in L.A. When are you coming?"

"To L.A.?"

"Yes dear, I hear you're absolutely FABULOUS."

"Really?!" I was always thrilled to hear that anyone was saying anything nice about me. "Who did you hear that from?"

"Natalie Cole!" she gushed. "Before she goes on, she can hear the audience HOWLING, even from her dressing room—she says she's NEVER heard anything like it!"

"That's really nice of her," I said—and I meant it.

"So when are you gonna come out here?" she asked, "So I can make a star out of you already."

I was totally blindsided by that one.

"Well...." I stuttered, "I was planning on being there, uhhhhhhhhh, Thursday?"

I'm going through nonexistent flight schedules in my head, thinking if I had wings at that exact moment, I'd have flown to this woman's office directly from the phone booth. She made it sound like my stardom was a foregone conclusion—just waiting for me to arrive at her doorstep and claim it.

I booked a flight and took my first trip to L.A. I stayed at the Westin Bonaventure Downtown. That shows how green I was—it was so far from the real action in Hollywood, I might as well have been staying in Nebraska. Somehow, I maneuvered my rental car to William Morris on El Camino Drive in Beverly Hills. I couldn't wait to get to Jenny Delaney—the woman who was going to make me a star. I parked and bounded into the office, gave the receptionist my name, and then settled into the comfy leather chairs waiting to be ushered up to the future.

You can tell how important you are by how long people allow you to languish in the lobby. You're at your hottest, with the shortest wait times, maybe twice in the relationship—in the beginning, when they think they can make you hot, and later, if lightning strikes and you actually ARE hot. At all other times in your career, you sit and wait while other *newly hot* or *actually hot* people get in before you do—either to discuss a project or have some expensive smoke blown up their asses.

That day I sailed right in to Ms. Delaney's office and got my first *Mwah! Mwah!* kiss on both cheeks. *What are we, in Paris?* The next half hour was her talking about how *hot* and *amazing* I was and that I'd be meeting with every network and studio in town. We would sift through all of the offers and decide who was going to have the privilege of being in the *Sarge Business*. She ended her monologue by looking me deep in the eye,

"Tell me," she said, with great pseudo-sincerity, "Are you ready?"

The only answer I could come up with, was, "Absolutely."

"Great," she said, "Let's get going! I want you to go across the street and meet everyone in the music department. They can't WAIT to meet you!"

Wow. *More people who can't wait to meet me, who I don't even know yet!* An assistant brought me across El Camino Drive to the *other* William Morris building, and the music department. All of the biggest stars in adult contemporary music were represented by William Morris, and I mean just about everybody. The assistant led me right into the head honcho's office—absolutely NO waiting.

"Hi, Sarge, Rob Heller. We can't wait to load you up with gigs."

I knew I was in the music department, because literally everything he was saying was music to my ears. We spent an hour talking about all of the big stars who couldn't wait to have me as their opening act, and he was every bit as nice and down-to-earth as Conan in the New York office. I felt like I was floating. It was happening! THIS was the STAR TREATMENT. I was thrilled, excited, and thoroughly terrified. I had no idea whether I'd be able to live up to the hype.

Were they telling the truth? Was I really so *fabulously talented*? I mean, these people handled other performers the whole world knew to be *fabulously* talented—did that mean maybe I was too? After I left William Morris, I called my managers, David and Christine Martin.

They were strangely unimpressed by my tales of the magical day at William Morris.

"Those people are just blowing smoke up your ass," said David. They both had very distinctive Australian accents that made everything they said sound like a *pronouncement.*

"It's true," said Christine. "I doubt they can put together an actual booking schedule that reflects all that fake enthusiasm."

Their skepticism harpooned my high in seconds flat. But these were my managers, just doing their job to *protect* me.

What if they were right? The seed of doubt they planted would have terrible consequences.

I made the rounds—taking all the meetings William Morris set up for me—being golf carted around studio lots meeting studio heads, and making my way around all the television network development executives. I had so many espressos and spring waters on those rounds, I still haven't had a good night's sleep and that was twenty years ago. By the third day, we were meeting with HBO at their tower in Century City. It was me, Lowell Mate, the head of HBO Studios, Jenny Delaney from William Morris, and my managers, David and Christine Martin.

Jenny ran the conversation. She was intent on setting me up with Martin Lawrence's producer, Samm-Art Williams.

"We have to create a vehicle for Sarge that captures his huge personality!" she said. "We want to showcase his quick wit, and his bi-racial ability to say things that singular ethnics just can't."

PERFECT, right?

My managers didn't say much in the meeting, but it seemed like we were cookin' with gas. After the meeting broke I went back with the Martins to their office—where they basically ripped apart the rationale for all of Jenny Delaney's plans that we had discussed at HBO.

But they would fix all of it.

They were my managers. I should trust them. I felt lucky. They were protecting me, right? The following week, David and Christine took me back to HBO. We went up to the same office, in the same tower, to see Lowell Mate. All of us were there again—except Jenny Delaney. I didn't know why she wasn't there, but I didn't think to interrupt the meeting and call her to discuss it. My managers had set this up and I trusted them unequivocally.

After some perfunctory conversation about the weather and other comedians, Lowell came from around the desk and extended his hand to me.

"I'm proud to be in the *Sarge Business*!" he said. "We're gonna do great things, I'll send the contract over to David and Christine later today."

Wow. HBO was in the *Sarge Business* with ME!

I got back to my hotel to find four messages from Jenny Delaney at William Morris. I called to tell her the good news about HBO. But it wasn't good news to her. She was livid.

"How did you make a deal with HBO?" she demanded to know, "What is the deal for? Who is the deal with? What are they going to pay you? What are you going to be doing with them?"

I couldn't answer ANY of those questions—I had no idea that Jenny wasn't part of making the deal—so I just told her to call my managers.

Apparently, she did, and it didn't go well.

We set an appointment, and I went over to William Morris to meet with Jenny. I waited in the lobby for over an hour. *Languished* would be a better term.

A few days earlier it was, "Go right up, they're expecting you."

Today it was, "I don't know, Sarge, I'll try Jenny again and let her know you're STILL here."

The receptionist finally told me to go on up. This time there was no assistant ushering me. I got out of the elevator and made my way down the hall, and spotted one of the other agents I'd met. On earlier visits, the agent greeted me with a loud, "SARGE!" This time, when that agent saw me, she quickly ducked down another corridor. It felt weird to be avoided so obviously by people who only last week were welcoming me like I'd won a war or something.

I made it to Jenny Delaney's office. All traces of the *Mwah! Mwah!* lady I'd met when I first got into town were gone. She was furious.

"How could you make this deal without me?! What makes you think I'd work this deal for you when you went behind my back?!"

I had no answers.

I thought she HAD been part of making the HBO deal. It didn't occur to me that she hadn't been, and I wouldn't have dreamed of cutting her out of anything. But somehow I couldn't make that clear to her. I still wanted to believe my managers were working for my best interests, so I couldn't out-and-out blame them.

It was getting very messy.

The next day, I was back at William Morris with my managers in a conference room with Jenny. David and Christine had told me to sit, listen, and learn from them. I was shocked at the contentiousness of the conversation. My managers basically declared war on my agents, accusing William Morris of trying to commandeer everything and take all the credit for everything. Uncharacteristically for me, I stayed silent. But inside, my mind was churning.

Wait a second. Isn't the whole point of this to get me successful? Who cares who gets the credit? I thought we were doing this to get a TV show and nurture and foster my career to some modicum of stardom.

Did I miss something?

This seemed like it was more about THEM, and less about ME.

I didn't know what to do. But regardless of whether my managers or my agents were in the right, there was an HBO deal on the table, and I wasn't about to let that go. When HBO sent the contract to David and Christine, I signed it.

I figured they would smooth things over somehow with William Morris.

I was wrong.

From that moment forward, I was *persona non grata* in the television office of my own agents because of this egregiously boneheaded play by my managers. That part of my relationship with William Morris died that day. Thank God Conan and the music department were still on my side, and the live music appearance part of my career continued to blossom.

Looking back, I can see that my managers' style was catastrophically counterproductive. They destroyed any chance that I had to become the television star these other powerful people were claiming I could become. My mistake. I listened to the negative people instead of the positive ones. That one is on me, not them. The hype was so huge from the agent side and the dourness so palpable from the manager side. If I could change one thing in my life, all things considered, I would have fired my managers and listened to my agents.

All that buzz evaporated and though I've worked steadily, in some ways, my career never recovered. The HBO deal never came to anything, and my television stardom ended before it began. But as I said, the live performance side was starting to take off—so I didn't have much time to sit and lick my wounds.

LOVE TO LOVE YOU BABY

There has always been a certain kismet to my life and career—a weird alignment of things and cosmic coincidences.

I don't actually think they are coincidences at all.

Which takes me to Radio City Music Hall.

I was still in Los Angeles, and I happened to be reading Sammy Davis, Jr.'s authorized bio *Yes I Can*. I love show business biographies. They help me feel connected to the greats, and I find so many parallels with the careers and lives of people who've come before me. Sometimes, there would be direct connections.

So, there I was at the gym, on the Stairclimber, tearing through *Yes I Can*, amazed at the parallels. Sammy and I had more in common than just the Black Jewish thing—we shared a lot of the same struggles. I was digging the part of the story where Sammy, his father, and his uncle—as the Will Mastin Trio—got their big break as Frank Sinatra's opening act in New York at Radio City Music Hall in 1949 or 1950.

One night during the run, Sinatra popped his head into their dressing room and asked if they needed anything. Sammy told Sinatra that every night after the show they had to schlep to New Jersey to a flophouse to sleep—wouldn't it be wonderful if Sinatra could get them rooms in New York City. Blacks weren't allowed to stay in most hotels in New York to that point.

Sinatra boldly told Sammy, "Done. Go to the Warwick Hotel tonight after the show and tell them I sent you."

So after the show, the trio hoofed it over to the Warwick Hotel from Radio City. As they appeared in front of the check-in desk, the clerk was short with them

"We've already filled the porter and shoe shine positions."

"We're Mr. Sinatra's friends," said Sammy, "And we'd like to check into our rooms, please, my kind sir."

The clerk swallowed a billiard ball of crow—or as it turned out,

Jim Crow—*sorry I couldn't resist*—and proceeded to check the Will Mastin Trio into the rooms reserved by Frank Sinatra. It was one of the first incidences of blacks being allowed to stay in a hotel in New York.

Black Jew, Radio City, Warwick Hotel...

After reading about all of that, I got off the Stairclimber, left the gym, and hopped in my car. My phone was dead, so I plugged it into the car charger. Once it got some juice it lit up. I had five messages, and four of them were from Conan, my guy in the New York William Morris office. I got him on the line as quickly as I could.

"Can you be on the red-eye?"

"Yeah, why?"

"You're opening for Donna Summer tomorrow night."

"WOW, really? Where?"

"Radio City Music Hall."

"Wow, I was just reading about—"

"Red-eye in, and a car service will pick you up to take you directly to Radio City to meet Donna Summer and her people. Then the car will take you to your hotel."

"Where am I staying?" I asked, venturing hopefully, "The Warwick?"

"Yeah," he said, "How did you know that?"

"I was just reading about my own life in someone else's book and it's a long story..."

I was blown away. I'm still blown away and it was nineteen years ago. These type of coincidences punctuate my life all the time, but never as thoroughly as that one. It blew my mind as profoundly as the night my addiction to drugs and alcohol died. I was struck by the lightning of coincidence. These occurrences are inspirational on so many levels. They reaffirm the destiny of the universe's presence in my life. They connect the dots, and make me look for other meaningful parallels.

It was show time at Radio City.

I was supposed to do thirty minutes before Donna Summer did her ninety-minute extravaganza of disco anthems and standards. My dressing room was on the third floor of Radio City, and it was crowded with the umbrellas and trench coats of all the agents that made their way over from the office to wish me well. On that night, nine agents introduced themselves to me as *my agent* at William Morris, chief among them, Kenny DiCamillo, a wonderful, funny, ungainly sort of character, with a scratchy voice and a heart of gold. It was impossible to feel not taken care of when Kenny was on the case.

I got the knock on my door for ten minutes, and having already done my prayers and meditation, I wasn't waiting for the five minute knock. I made my way down to the stage and got myself ready for the most exhilarating, scary, unbelievable stand-up comedy experience of my career.

I'd only been doing stand-up full time since February, 1992. It was July 7, 1996—four and a half years from Ted's couch to the home of the Rockettes. Meteoric in show business terms. Most entertainers NEVER get this far, but there I was. The countdown to show time had begun and I was taken by a stagehand to my mark, and was told that when the countdown had begun, it could not be stopped, and that I shouldn't start performing until my entire body was clear of the city block-wide curtain which would take a full minute to unfurl.

A FULL MINUTE!

While I waited nervously on my mark, a high caliber intestinal event started beckoning. A fart. At least I thought it was a fart. As I squirmed to give the gas its freedom, it became obvious that it was neither gaseous nor liquid but solid. Very solid. *And it wasn't going to be stopped.* I screamed to the stage hand, "Stop the countdown!"

I ran off stage right and frantically asked for directions to the nearest bathroom.

"Up in your dressing room."

I'd never make the three flights let alone two more steps. He pointed to a stage-side slop sink. I undid my pants, hung my ass into the sink, and a dollop of clean, dry poop fell out. I turned on the faucet, rinsed my butt, and pulled my pants back up. I always perform *commando* (sans underwear) and lucky I do, because briefs would have complicated things. I ran back to my mark and my patent leather Doc Martens were shiny with Radio City stage light, then my legs, then my hands, my chest and finally I was fully revealed. I made it in time—poop and all. Radio City was gigantic. I was performing comedy but I couldn't hear the laughter. In comedy clubs and smaller venues, the laughter gets projected up to the stage. At Radio City on this night, I just couldn't hear anything. I finished my set, and as I left the stage, the agents mobbed me. They were ecstatic, telling me how I slaughtered the crowd, and that they loved me. But I wasn't feeling it. I was afraid I'd bombed—and the poop thing happening hadn't exactly helped boost my confidence level.

Kenny approached me last.

"You didn't unpack yet, did you?" he asked, "Because Wayne Newton loves you."

I was shocked. "Wayne Newton? How does he even know who I am?"

"He listened to your set," he said, "I had my phone open and he wants you to come to Myrtle Beach and work with him."

I was floored. Fresh off what I thought was the bomb of all bombs I was already booked to work with *Mr. Las Vegas*. I was confused.

"What about Donna Summer?"

"Oh, you have the tour," Kenny said. "Thirty-six cities. They already booked it—they just wanted you tonight at Radio City too."

I have the tour already? I'm going to Myrtle Beach to open for Wayne-O? Somebody pinch me. I'll be right back, I'm just going to the slop sink backstage to put the shit back in my ass so I can shit again.

I went back to the hotel, grabbed my luggage, and caught the last flight that night from LaGuardia to South Carolina through Atlanta. I'd just *slayed 'em* at the most prestigious theater in the world, and I was on my way to work with Wayne Newton. Amazing. I got to Myrtle Beach and the next day I went to the Palace Theater. I always get to gigs extra early so I can relax and do my spiritual preparation—basically, pray my ass off that I don't lay an egg. I was in my dressing room. There was the thirty-minute-to-show knock. Then fifteen. Then ten. A minute after the ten knock, there was another knock.

"I fucking heard you, ten minutes." I yelled.

Wearing only a towel and shoes I pulled the door open to yell at whoever was annoying me. I flung the door open and it was HIM. Wayne Newton, in the flesh, in a satin robe with *Wayne-O* embroidered on the breast pocket. I was embarrassed, shocked, and frozen all at the same time.

"I'm so sorry, Mr. Newton, I thought…"

"Don't be silly, Sarge, I just wanted to come say hey and check in with you and make sure you have everything you need." He said, "Plus, I wanted to find out if it's okay if I introduce you as my co-star tonight."

"Uhhhhhhhhhhh, sure, yeah, right," I fumbled, "Your co-star, that's, okay, yes, great, thank you."

I must have sounded like a moron.

"C'mere, Hombre," he said, "Gimme a show biz hug."

We embraced and now I really had to hurry. Another knock.

"Five minutes, Sarge."

I went out and I thought I *slayed 'em*. I felt as good about my set as I ever had—certainly better than I'd felt at Radio City. I got back to the hotel and I was halfway through a Diet Coke when the phone rang.

"Hey, Killer, Wayne here. I'm terribly sorry but it's just not going to work out," *What?!* "But you'll be paid for the week," he continued, "And hopefully we'll have you out to the ranch, and you can work the Vegas shows with me."

I had what I thought was the kiss of death set at Radio City but was booked for a tour with Donna Summer, and I had what I thought was a monster set, but got fired.

What I thought was of no consequence.

I had to learn to stop thinking, stop judging, stop evaluating my performances and just let them be whatever they were as I moved forward.

I went on tour with Donna Summer from the summer of 1996 to the spring of 1997—the greatest learning experience of my performing life—the Ohio State Fair competing with the sound of the cattle auction on the other side of the event space, Las Vegas, Chicago, Detroit—I was everywhere and loved every second of it. We were in Atlanta at Chastain Park at the exact moment people were being evacuated from the Olympic Village because of that imbecile who bombed the place. (That night, the event producer gave me Donna's paycheck accidentally. I opened the envelope. It was for close to a quarter million dollars. Though I had a fleeting fantasy of leaving the tour and moving to Peru, I gave back the check.

We made most of the tour dates by bus, and found ourselves with a couple of down days in Indianapolis before doing two concerts there. Much deserved R&R for the musicians and weary crew. I was in my hotel room when there was a knock on the door. It was Donna Summer.

"Nobody wants to go shopping with me, Freckles," she said. "Will you come?" She was adorable. Off I went shopping with Donna Summer, to an upscale downtown Indy mall, where we ended up at the Designer Collections department of Nordstrom's. I stood by like a bodyguard while the disco tornado ripped outfits from what seemed like every rack simultaneously. She found the outfits she liked—some Richard Tyler numbers—and looked at the tags.

"Get a pen and paper," she said to me, "And write these SKU numbers down."

"What's a SKU number?"

"The identification number of the garment," she said, "There's no way I'm paying Nordstrom's prices for this stuff when I can call Richard Tyler directly and have him send the stuff over. But I need the SKU numbers so they know what to send."

That was for the expensive designer stuff. In other parts of the store, there turned out to quite a few things though that Donna was willing to actually purchase that day, and my arms were draped with tons of clothes. Almost like someone who's at the end of a run on drugs, virtually out of breath from her shopping frenzy, she stopped.

"Let's go, Freckles."

We got to the register and she impatiently continued to work the racks near the counter while the girl was carefully folding and ringing each item. At some point Donna turned back to me.

"Are you enjoying opening for the concerts?" she asked.

"This is the highlight of my life," I said. I wasn't sucking up, just being honest. The salesgirl was eavesdropping.

"Sorry, but I overheard you say that you're doing concerts." The young clerk, probably a college student, turned to Donna. "Ma'am, it's an honor to have you in our city. Are the PIPS traveling with you too?"

And that was that.

"Let's go, Freckles," Donna said—royally pissed at being mistaken for Gladys Knight—*do we really all look alike?* "Put down the stuff, put it down, and let's go." She grabbed my arm with such force, I was surprised my left arm wasn't torn out of the socket. That poor salesgirl had no idea what her mistake would cost Nordstrom's in sales.

When the tour ended, the William Morris agency had me working all the time—with Aretha, the Four Tops, the Temptations, The Beach Boys, Paul Anka, and Natalie Cole, among others. I was in pig heaven. Not all comedians could open for big acts, but I was big too—in size and personality—and I could OPEN for people. Plus, I didn't care that the audience wasn't there specifically to see me. I knew that from Heaven, my Poppy could see me.

THE MARTIN-MORRIS SHUFFLE

Things were great in New York with William Morris, but incredibly, I was still with my managers, David and Christine Martin.

Why? Why did I stay with them? Why did I listen?

Hindsight is twenty-twenty, and I have a theory: *Of course I stayed.* The agents told me how great I was, were nice to me, believed in me, and were kind.

Of course I didn't trust them.

My managers made me feel like shit, constantly told me I wasn't as good as I thought I was, and made it clear I was the low man on their comedy totem pole.

Of course I believed they were right.

My physical addiction may have disappeared in one night.

My self-loathing and conditioning was another story entirely.

In a power play, the Martins pulled all thirteen of their clients from William Morris. They worked me.

Things weren't what they seemed at William Morris, and if I stayed, I'd be committing career suicide—I felt like I had no choice but to call my man Conan Smith, who had been nothing but a mensch *to* me and *for* me, and leave the agency.

Working with Conan felt good, so it must be bad.

Working with David and Christine Martin felt bad, so it must be good. On some level I knew I was making one of the biggest mistakes of my life, but I felt powerless to make any other choice. I say now that I didn't have the show business instincts at the time to understand how I should have listened to what my gut was telling me—but I kind of think that's horseshit. *I didn't have the HUMAN instincts.* I didn't believe in myself enough as a person, to believe what my heart was telling me. Sure, I was strong-armed by managers, but I knew it was wrong, so ultimately, the onus is on me forever.

Conan tried to stop me. "Your managers are the problem," he

correctly pointed out, "Not us."

But I left him. And I don't think he will ever forgive or forget. I've tried in subsequent years to make amends, but he's never once returned one of my calls. That's as clear as it gets: *You're dead to me.* I don't blame him. I blame myself.

But who was my new agent going to be?

I was out with friends at Jerry's Famous Deli across from Cedars-Sinai Hospital slurping a bowl of the best matzo ball noodle soup in Los Angeles, when four young men in white shirts and dark ties inched over to our table. They were all probably named Josh or Matt.

"Are you Sarge?" one of them asked.

"Yeah," I said, "Who's asking?"

He turned to the others.

"I told you it was him."

Then back to me.

"Hey man, I'm Matt," he said. *Of course you are,* "And we're really looking forward to working with you."

"Who are you?"

"We're ICM," he said, like it should have been obvious to me. "We saw your tape in our bi-coastal morning talent meeting and it was unanimous."

"Really?" I said, "What was unanimous?"

"You're the SHIT!" Said Matt with a grin. "You are hilarious!"

They all started punching me playfully in a kind of corporate lockstep.

"You're the SHIT!" they all echoed.

"We're really looking forward to when you come over on Tuesday," one of the other ones piped in.

"TUESDAY." I said. *This was surreal.* "Okay guys, well I guess I'll see you Tuesday. Thanks for coming over."

They were right. The Martins had made the appointment. And come Tuesday afternoon I found myself in a conference room a few blocks over from William Morris, at ICM—a huge marble fortress that looked like a mausoleum. My manager, Christine, and I walked into a huge conference room and there were like eighteen people around the table waiting, legal pads in front of them, pencils poised to write— I have no idea what.

"What is all this?" I asked her in a nervous whisper.

"They're signing you," she said.

Okay. But something told me inside that I was going from the Yankees to the Mets—a step down—this is not to cast any aspersion on what ICM was at this time, but I was loved at William Morris, and these people were... strange. At least I recognized Matt and his cohorts from Jerry's, at the far end of the table on one of the corners. Apparently they weren't THE SHIT at ICM, and didn't rate prime seats at this pow-wow.

I broke the silence.

"So, what are we waiting for?"

As the words left my mouth an attractive, dark haired, woman in patent leather Prada driving shoes bounded into the room.

"There he is!" she said, pointing to me, "THE STAR!"

She stuck her hand out.

"Leigh, Leigh Brillstein," she said, "And I promise you, we're gonna fuckin' embarrass the shit out of William Morris."

Thus began a torrent of four-letter words—I'm no stranger to cursing, but this woman sounded like a truck driver—*not to impugn the sensitivities of truck drivers...* She made some grandiose claims about how great it was going to be for me at ICM, and then someone produced a thick, thick stack of paper which apparently was my contract.

Everyone looked at me. I was supposed to sign it.

So I signed.

I didn't take it home and read it. I didn't ask to leave the room and call my lawyer. I signed. I didn't really know what I was signing, but based on the way my career went from that moment forward, I'm guessing ICM wrote it up something like this: *ICM hereby agrees to create no employment opportunities for Sarge a.k.a. Steven Pickman ("The Artist"), and in furtherance of this goal, ICM warrants that they will make all reasonable efforts to ensure that career prospects for The Artist will diminish until such time as he desires to quit show business entirely and seek employment in another field more suited to his particular skills.*

Like maybe working as a CVS stock boy.

At William Morris I worked. At ICM I was non-existent immediately following the giant meeting with eighteen people who thought I was the SHIT. I became invisible to all of the Matts and Joshes, and especially to Leigh Brillstein who apparently had other clients to entertain with four-letter words.

But I never stopped trying to make my own opportunities, and Cosmic Coincidence reared her gorgeous head again about a year and a half after I joined ICM—when I hadn't worked much, and that stock boy job at CVS was looking tempting.

Craig Shoemaker, a juggernaut comedy club comic and a good friend, was hired to sidekick on *The Magic Hour*—Magic Johnson's ill-fated late night talk show. Craig had been invited to perform for a huge charity event in Bermuda—Samuel L. Jackson's personal foundation to help women and children—but because of *The Magic Hour*, he needed to find a replacement for the gig in Bermuda. He graciously asked me to do it. What seemed like moments later, I was on a charter flight with two hundred television and film stars heading for Bermuda. It seemed like I was the only non-celebrity on the flight. Everywhere I turned—Denzel, Michael Douglas, Samuel L. and his wife, Dustin Hoffman and on and on and on.

We got to Bermuda, and it turns out there's four days of golfing before the show. I don't play golf. So I spent those four days on Elbow Beach with the celebrity wives—cracking them up left and right and having a ball. In the evenings, all these famous men were coming up to me.

"My wife says you're hilarious!"

"I hope you're as funny Saturday night as you've been during the day."

It was all ribbing and in great fun.

Saturday night arrived and I was excited. I was scheduled on the line-up between Mike Orenstein, and the great Jim Breuer—then hot off *SNL*. It was an outdoor show in front of thousands of people. The first four rows were all of the celebrities I'd traveled with.

No pressure, right.

There was no backstage, but there were bushes on the berm above the stage and we sat back there right before show time. I'm there, Orenstein's there, but no Jim Breuer. They start the show Mike Orenstein goes up first. While Orenstein was on, Jim Breuer stumbles out of the bushes, a *Dark and Stormy* (half dark rum, half Bermudian beer) in each hand. *Shitfaced. Slaughtered.* I loved Jim and still do. He's sweet-natured and wildly talented. But that was not a good night for him.

"How much time can you do?" he slurred, in a barely intelligible whisper.

"An hour," I said, "Maybe an hour and twenty."

"Good," he said, "Do it. Because I don't think I can talk."

Orenstein did great and then Samuel L. Jackson introduced me. I came out and just murdered the joint. I had the greatest time of my life. There was a piano and I used the piano, and I made fun of the celebrities, and Bermuda's pink beaches. You name it, I slammed it— and I got a standing ovation. Breuer came out for five minutes and did this hilarious thing with hand puppets of different animals while laying down on top of the piano. Which was a good thing, because I don't think he could have stood up.

Afterwards, I was surrounded by well-wishers and celebrities gushing that I stole the show and I was funnier than they'd heard about all week. I heard that siren song again—that I was going to be a star. People kept asking me the same question.

"Has Tony Howard found you yet?"

I'm thinking, who the fuck is Tony Howard? And if he wants to find me so badly, well, we're on an island, I'm not going anywhere. How hard can it be?

The Tony Howard thing went on through the evening. I went to bed that night, and in my pre-bed prayers, I found myself asking God to please send Tony Howard to me, whoever he was, so I'd stop hearing his name.

The next day E! Entertainment asked me to do interviews of the celebrities at the golf tournament which was culminating that day. I gladly agreed, and for the first time of the trip, I actually went to the country club. All morning I did my best to create funny on-camera bits with the celebrities. At lunch I was getting chummy with all of my new celebrity friends, when I felt a tap on my shoulder. I turned around and saw no one standing there until I looked down. There was an adorable woman with a boy cut and glasses.

She extended her tiny little hand up to me.

"I'm Toni Howard."

"Oh my God!" I said, "You're Toni Howard. I thought you were some guy looking for me."

"I AM looking for you." She said, "But I'm not just some guy, I'm THE guy."

Then what came after that was a barrage of compliments about how amazing and talented and funny I was, and how I was going to be huge star. *The usual.*

"Thank you," I said, "That's a nice compliment."

"I'm gonna sign you right now and make you HUGE!" she said with a glint in her eye, "You know you're gonna be huge honey, you know that don't you?"

"Well," I said, "What are you signing me to do?"

She turned to her friend.

"Isn't he adorable," she said, "With the freckles and the…"

What is she signing me to?

"Do you work for an agency? What am I signing?"

She took a napkin from the bar and a pen.

"Trust me," she said, handing me the pen, "Sign this and you'll never regret it."

She was very convincing. I signed my name on the napkin.

"Now that I signed," I said, "Can I ask, who are you with?"

"Honey, I'm not WITH anyone," she said. "I *RUN* ICM."

I laughed really hard.

"ICM?" I said, "Like the *agency* ICM, with the marble lobby on Wilshire?"

"That's right."

I kept laughing.

"Why are you laughing?" she wanted to know.

"Because," I said, "I'm already SIGNED WITH ICM."

Her jaw dropped.

"What are you talking about you're *WITH ICM*." She said, "How come I've never heard of you?"

"I don't know why you've never heard of me," I said, "But I've been with ICM for a year and a half and haven't had one audition, not one stitch of work through you guys, NADA."

Now she was kind of pissed.

"I'm going to get to the bottom of this you can bet on that," she said, "This is preposterous. You are the funniest, the cutest, the most talented act I've seen in years and everybody here thinks so. Call me Monday when we get back to Los Angeles."

I called Toni Howard Monday.

I called Toni Howard Tuesday.

I called Toni Howard Wednesday.

I called Toni Howard Thursday.

Finally, Thursday at dinner time, my phone rang,

"Please hold, I have Toni Howard for you."

"Sarge, Toni Howard. I've done some investigating and I'm afraid the news isn't good. I spoke to your agent and the head of the department, and the reason why you've had such a rough go of it at ICM is because of how difficult you are for people to work with."

"WHAT?" I gasped, "Difficult to work with?"

I was too flabbergasted to keep my anger and frustration out of my voice.

"I HAVEN'T WORKED WITH *ANYBODY*, IN OR OUT OF YOUR COCKAMAMIE AGENCY SINCE I SIGNED WITH YOU!" *Was I yelling? I don't know.* "At William Morris I worked, all the time, at YOUR agency, that you RUN, I spoke to you longer at the golf course in Bermuda than all of the conversations with my agents added up."

Dead silence on the other end.

"Thank you for getting to the bottom of this," I said, and hung up.

Two weeks later I left ICM.

I was down but not out.

ROMANCE ON THE HIGH SEAS

I was knocking around L.A. without a job, when a friend of mine told me about cruise ships and put me in touch with an agent in Florida that books comedians for several cruise lines. It paid better than comedy clubs, you got to go to all kinds of gorgeous locales all over the world, and you worked full-size theaters.

I'm a big guy. I like big rooms.

How could I go wrong?

By then I was living in a shabby garden apartment with guys who smoked crack in the next room—while I was still sober, and still going to two recovery meetings a day.

I had loved living in Los Angeles, but if you're in show business and you're not *killing it* in the biz, L.A. is a hard place to be. Plus I needed to make a living. I started working here and there for Norwegian, Royal Caribbean, and Princess Cruise lines. The pay was great, the theaters were full, and the locations were exotic.

I even got to meet one of my idols, Don Rickles. I was the headliner comedian in the theater when I found out that he and his wife were going to be passengers. I was paralyzed with excitement and fear at the thought of Don Rickles seeing me perform—excitement because I knew I was a good enough comic and was stoked that I'd have a chance to meet him—but terrified by the thought that I might bomb the night he's in the audience.

Maybe he won't want to be bothered to come see some schleppy comic on his vacation.

I'd already performed on board a couple of nights before Rickles and his wife Barbara got on the ship. I was fortunate enough to get a standing ovation. When you're a funny comic on a cruise ship, everyone on board is aware of you and if the show is good enough they're buzzing at breakfast and lunch the next day. In a way, you're like a celebrity onboard, but Rickles, a REAL celebrity, was coming aboard. As I made my way around the ship I was rehearsing to myself what I'd say to Rickles when I met him.

My grandpa Herman knew you from the Friars Club in New York.

No, I don't want to make him feel older than he already is by bringing up my dead Poppy. Hmmmm.

You're my idol sir and I started doing stand-up immediately after I got out of rehab.

No, I can't say that. I resolved to just stick my hand out like everyone else and tell him how much I loved his work.

Later that day, I was by the front desk, and I saw him! There he was! My mother's favorite comic and the reason I was bitten with the bug at six in the Playhouse at Grossinger's so many years ago. He was talking to an older woman, and could hear what she was saying.

"Have you seen Sarge?" she asked *Don Rickles*. "What a comedian. I laughed 'til I cried at his show the other night. Have you seen him?"

"No," Rickles said, a smile pasted on his face, "I haven't had the pleasure but everyone keeps asking me about him."

Great! The man's on vacation and people keep asking him about me.

Instead of going over and introducing myself, I snuck away in the other direction, postponing the inevitable. I knew I'd eventually have to meet him—we're on a floating building surrounded by water, where's he gonna go?

Later that night I was at dinner, and my table was situated several tables from the host station at the entrance. In walks Don Rickles and his wife. I see him smile and I put my head down. I don't know why. He wouldn't know me even if we were in a phone booth together.

But he says to the maître d' in a voice everyone could hear, "Can I sit at Sarge's table, put us with Sarge, I want to sit with Sarge."

I almost died. All eyes in the dining room were on him and he was literally shouting, "Where's Sarge? I want to sit with Sarge." I held my napkin over the lower half of my face as the maître d' whisked him and his wife past. I was just too embarrassed. I finished my meal and went back to my cabin.

The next night was show night. I was wracked with fear because I hadn't seen Rickles since the night before in the dining room. Now I'm backstage waiting for my introduction. I hear the cruise director say my intro.

"He's a hilarious comedy sensation, direct from Vegas!"

Direct from Vegas.

It's an intro all cruise directors use for entertainers to make the audience think they're really seeing somebody special.

Rickles is direct from Vegas, I'm not direct from Vegas. Oh my God, he's gonna tell everyone that he's never heard of me in Vegas.

I come out and the audience is applauding. I start my set and about ten minutes in, I notice someone coming from the left side of the theater and up the steps to the stage at a really quick pace.

It was Rickles!

He came up the steps, on stage, screaming, "Has anyone seen Sarge, anyone, anyone at all. I'm looking for Sarge?"

I looked over my left shoulder and then over my right as he went off the other side of the stage down the steps and back into the house.

The audience howled. We kibitzed back and forth. He was such a great sport. So generous. I'd been an idiot to run away in the dining room.

"Sarge!" he kept yelling, putting the audience in stiches.

"Karaoke's on Friday night pal!" I finally told him, wrapping up our impromptu bit, "This stage is for funny people!"

The audience howled again. It was a great line for a great man.

But it wasn't all about comedy aboard ship.

While onboard the S.S. Norway I was in the back of the theater one night watching the production cast do *Chicago*. I was kibitzing with John Ferrentino, my lifelong entertainer pal, a comedian who does magic. Ferrentino had ridden the comedy boom of the '80s, and had done over a hundred television appearances and we were performing in the same lounge on the ship. If performing on ships was good enough for him, it was good enough for me.

We were watching the show from the back row, standing next to the spotlight operator, and I fell in love. Right there from the back of the theater, four hundred feet away. There were eight dancers on stage and I only saw one. I told myself I'd marry her if I got the chance. I don't know why I thought that but it would prove to be prophetic. I couldn't think of anything but her. I didn't know her name but I was going to meet this girl. I knew she was aware of me because I spotted her at the back of one of my shows with a friend of hers.

But how would I meet my future wife?

I went to every one of her shows and sat in the theater long after the audience left hoping for an encounter, anything, a conversation. I did this for a couple of weeks until my perseverance paid off. One night after the show, I was sitting alone in the theater. Everyone seemed to be gone from backstage until SHE appeared with a gym bag slung over her shoulder, in sweats, with her falsies still on.

I stuttered through an introduction.

"I'm Sssssssarge."

"I know." She said, "Why are you still here?"

"Because I was hoping I would run into you."

Her name was Fiona.

Fiona and I sat in the theater, just the two of us and talked for four hours. This was the beginning of a romance that would culminate in a long distance relationship by mail. It was complicated because she lived in a hostel in London's Notting Hill and I lived in Los Angeles. We spoke on the phone every other night and wrote each other every day. I didn't want to be the reason she broke up with her boyfriend, Andy in London, so I made it crystal clear that I wanted her to come and visit with me in L.A. but only if things with Andy were finished.

In April of 1999, Fiona came to visit and never left. We were madly in love and had the greatest time together. I was living in Hollywood and she moved in with me when it became clear that it didn't seem like she would get tired of hanging out with a guy fifteen years her senior.

Did I mention she was just twenty-four years old?

We traveled the country together, and on ships we traveled the world. Every time we came home though, we longed for a life on land where we both could do our show biz things—me comedy, she dancing. Fiona only had an H-1 visa—and its expiration date was rapidly approaching.

"Just keep auditioning for things," I said, "Worry about the visa thing IF they offer you the job."

But I was wrong. Again and again she auditioned and they wanted her, but she couldn't be hired because of her immigration status. We tried every way short of getting married to wangle a green card for her, including retaining a top immigration attorney.

"Do you love each other?" he asked. "Why don't you just get married?"

On Labor Day weekend in 1999 we eloped to Las Vegas and got married downtown at the court house, dressed in our workout clothes. She looked so young. There wasn't a casino in Las Vegas we went to that week where she didn't get carded—usually they thought her ID was fake, and we would be asked to leave.

All of my friends in Florida, where I got sober, my family in New York, and my homeys in L.A. gave me a resounding thumbs up.

Fiona was beautiful, funny, and we were very much in love.

I liked that my guy friends would whisper to me that I was their hero for landing a gorgeous, young babe, and that her British accent was adorable.

Finally I was THE MAN.

BIO-MOM

I had never really felt a desire to find my biological mother. I also never fully realized its psychological importance. But an encounter with a TV producer at a party at Bryan Callen's house in Venice pushed me to make an effort. (Among other very funny roles in film and TV, Bryan played the Middle Eastern wedding chaplain in *The Hangover*.)

I was talking with Gil Junger Witt (a creator and producer of legendary sitcoms in the '70s and '80s like *Soap* and *The Golden Girls*). When he heard about my whole Black/Jewish/Adopted thing, he had a strong reaction.

"You have to find your real mother," he said. "YOU HAVE TO!"

All I knew about her was that she was an Orthodox Jew from Chicago, and I knew her name. My curiosity about her had never reached a level that made me do anything, until my conversation at that party with Gil. Maybe God doesn't speak directly to us anymore like in the Old Testament when he spoke to just about everyone in a booming voice from the heavens to do something biblical. But I believe he does speak to us through other people. When Gil was so persistent, it struck me that maybe there was a reason—maybe the universe was telling me something through him.

Maybe getting married and thinking more about family also played a part. But it also began to occur to me, that if I found my biological mother, I might know once and for all about my racial identity. I mean, by then I was assuming I was half Black, but was I? Were there other ethnicities involved?

Who am I, anyway?

I went online to do some research and found a company called Kinsolving. They promised to find anyone it was possible to find, with the caveat that if they did in fact find who you were looking for, you owed them thirty-nine hundred dollars.

So I filled out their questionnaire.

In a way, I hoped they'd find nothing—I mean, I was *curious* but not *almost four thousand bucks-curious*. Then I forgot about it—until one day I was in my stale apartment in L.A. talking to Fiona when the phone rang.

"Hello? Mr. Pickman, Steven Charles Pickman?" It was a feminine-sounding man from Kinsolving. "We've 'solved' your case!"

"What case?"

"You signed a contract with us to find your biological mother," he said. "And we've found her."

If I wanted the details I'd have to FedEx a check to him for the thirty-nine hundred. He would then email the information to me. My hands began to shake—not about the possibility of finding my birth mother—but about sending some guy four grand over the phone.

I didn't know what I was going to do, but I asked for the address and told him I would send out a check right away. The part of me that wanted to know about my bio-mom, was less skeptical than the part of me that had to figure out where I was going to find four grand. After sharing the news with Fiona, my next call was to my mother. I told her I needed thirty-nine hundred dollars, and that a company had located my birth mother.

"Are you sure you want to know?" she asked.

"Yes," I said.

She wrote the check and mailed it directly to Kinsolving.

Several days later, without any warning, an email from Kinsolving appeared in my inbox, listing names, dates of birth, and home phone number of about forty people they said I was related to, including my biological mother.

Was this even legal?

Apparently my mother's family were Russian Jews who immigrated to Winnipeg, Canada, and then moved to Chicago.

Now I was interested—but scared. Rather than just call my mother, I decided I'd call someone else on the list with a date of birth close to mine to try get a little info on my mother instead of just calling her out of the blue.

I found a cousin born a year after me and rang her up.

"Hello?"

"Hi, my name is Steven Pickman, and I got your number from a list I received from a company helping me to find my biological mother." I was talking like a caffeinated machine gun and it must have sounded like a scam or a crank call. "This company says my biological mother is your Aunt Susan. You have an Aunt Susan, right?"

There was a long pause.

"Who is this and why are you calling me?" She sounded pissed.

Not the response I was hoping for, but I repeated my whole spiel—*list, company, bio-mom, Aunt Susan.*

"I don't know who you are," she said, "But my Aunt Susan never married and never had any children."

I hadn't really thought about the fact that I might be sharing a family secret with someone who had no idea I had even been born.

"Well," I said, "I was given up for adoption by a young woman in 1961 and the company I hired to investigate has determined that your Aunt Susan is my biological mother."

The cousin was having none of it. I don't know if she thought I was lying, or if she just didn't want to get involved, but it was a dead end. I couldn't seem to make her understand that I wasn't looking to get anything from the situation. I just wanted to know my REAL ethnic background, and a little bit about the woman who gave birth to me.

I decided I'd have to bite the bullet and call my mother directly. I left messages at the two numbers I was given for her, one was in Illinois, the other in Las Vegas—but I didn't hear back.

That Labor Day weekend, I was appearing with Kevin Eubanks and Oleta Adams at Caesars Palace in Las Vegas. Fiona was sleeping face down on the chaise lounge next to me and from my chair I could see my name on the Caesar's Palace marquis in huge letters. SARGE. I wanted to call somebody and share how excited I was about the marquee, plus it was my birthday in a couple of days and I was so damn proud of appearing there. I scrolled through my phone looking for who to call, and my biological mother's Las Vegas phone number jumped out at me. Without thinking much about it, I dialed.

After several rings a voice answered.

"Hello?"

"Hello," I said. "Does the date June 1, 1961 mean anything to you?"

"Who is this?!" she angrily barked.

"My name is Steven Pickman," I said, "And from what I've learned through an investigative agency, you are my biological mother."

There was a long pause, maybe fifteen seconds.

"Where were you born?" she asked uneasily.

"Miami Beach," I said.

"What were your parents' names?"

"Francine and Chester Pickman."

Another long pause. Now I guess it was sinking in for her because her tone changed.

"I couldn't keep you," she said softly.

My compassion for her and what it must have been like for her as a single Jewish mother giving birth to a mixed-race baby in 1961 was already huge.

"I don't want anything from you," I said. "I have a life, and I have a wife, but I'm about to start a family of my own, and I had a really tough time not knowing anything about myself all these years." I went on, "I don't want to pass that same uncertainty on to MY children."

Again, there was a long pause.

"He was a Black man that I met in college," she said finally. "He was very musical. I don't remember his name, but the relationship didn't last that long."

That was it? A whole life of not knowing what I was or what the circumstances were of my origin, and that was all?

At that moment I felt some relief, but it wasn't like a huge weight had been lifted from my chest. I knew I wasn't White. That was obvious, right? I'd been performing as a "Black Jew" for years already, but touching base was comforting. I thanked her, told her I was grateful for all of her choices, and told her my website address in the event that she wanted to keep up with me from a distance. I also gave her my home phone number and thanked her again.

"Where are you?" she asked.

"Las Vegas."

She gasped. "What are you doing in Las Vegas?"

"I'm a comedian," I said, "I'm performing at Caesar's Palace."

"Do you have a stage name, not Steven Pickman?"

"Sarge."

"Oh my goodness, you're Sarge?"

"Yes I am."

"That's so funny," she said. "My friend and I were going to go to your show last night, but she was unwell, so we didn't go out."

"Well," I said, "If you'd like, I'll leave you tickets at will-call for the rest of the engagement. If you want to come see the show, just come."

We finished the call, and that was that. Every night after that, for the rest of my engagement, I left tickets as I'd promised, but each night I checked and no one claimed them.

It was okay.

I was okay.

I just hope that after I interrupted her life, that she'd be okay too.

SARGE IN THE FOXHOLE

For a couple of years things were great. I was going on ships—and then I tapped into some work that would change my life yet again. My friend Craig Shoemaker (the one who got me the Samuel L. Jackson gig in Bermuda) was hired to do a radio show on a new network that was creating programs with some of America's top club comics on an internet radio format. It was called Comedy World.

Craig asked me to be his sidekick. We loved performing together, and it should have gone great, from the night of our first demo show in a studio in Hollywood, the powers that be, Kent Emmons, a radio industry magnate, and Howard Weinstein, a bankruptcy attorney, began offering me my own show.

Because of my loyalty to *Shoe* (Shoemaker's nickname), I declined. I was there to support and sidekick Shoe. Period. I'd been screwed out of too many things by too many people to betray my friend. They asked again and again. Finally they made their final offer—they were firing Shoe anyway—so either I took a show of my own, or I'd be fired along with him.

I felt that I had no choice. I took the deal. The next day Shoe's show was canceled and I got a show with Mike Orenstein, the other comic from the Bermuda gig. The new show was *Sarge 'n Stein—The Monsters of the Night.*

Craig never forgave me.

Mike and I worked out of a warehouse studio in Marina del Rey, California, and I was making great money. The bosses must have liked the show because they offered me a second show on the weekends doing sports talk. To book guests for the sports show I drew upon my vast rolodex of sports people I'd worked with over the years at CBS, ABC, and ESPN. Giants Super Bowl star Phil Simms came on my show as did Greg Gumbel—apparently forgiving me for boosting money from him back in the day when I was still using—and many, many others. On Sundays I frequently had Chris Myers on with me and we'd goof around off the air about how much fun our days were in Bristol doing the two o'clock *Sportscenter* every morning. After about a month, Chris asked me if I'd like to co-host his show on the brand spanking new Fox Sports Radio. I accepted and it turned into a career maker for me. The second day while I was filling in with Chris for Steve Lyons, who was off somewhere doing Fox Baseball coverage, the president of Fox Sports, David Hill, came in to listen to the show from the control booth. During one of the commercial breaks, Hill motioned for me to come out of the booth. I went and met him and he was sitting with James Brown, the host of *Fox NFL Sunday*. I knew JB from my days at CBS.

"Son, you are a phenomenal performer," David Hill told me, "And you should have your own show here."

"Thank you," I said.

And I was given my own three-hour show following the co-host spot I was doing with Chris Myers. I'd never done radio before. I went from being a total novice to hosting fifty hours a week. I worked most days co-hosting with Chris from two to five, my own slot from five to eight, and then I'd rush over to Marina del Rey from the Fox offices in Rancho Park, to do my two hours of *Monsters of the Night* on Comedy World with Mike Orenstein. On Sunday I had my two-hour sports talk show, then three more hours on Fox Sports Radio.

Between the two networks, I was making a small fortune.

Then Jay Clark, the GM of Comedy World gave me an ultimatum. He said he couldn't have me working at two networks and that I'd have until the end of the conversation to pick one or the other. I'm a comedian, but I'm also a sports freak, and I didn't quite know if Comedy World's future was particularly secure.

I chose Fox.

For once, when forced to choose, it turned out that I made the right decision.

For two years I held down a three-hour show at Fox Sports Radio making occasional television appearances on *The Best Damn Sports Show Period*. I got moved up to the nightly eleven to two spot, and later, got a talented co-host, Jason Smith. Jason was an X's and O's guy with an encyclopedic mind for stats and numbers. Since he was from Staten Island and I was from Long Island, we were home boys, and we successfully created and performed an entertaining show called *Sarge in the Foxhole* on Fox Sports Radio. I loved coming to work with Jason and we were the only show live on-the-air the night after 9-11 happened.

The network had been preempted by Fox News all day until our show. We opened the show with the Whitney Houston singing of the Super Bowl and I remember it was emotional for us as New Yorkers, and even became more emotional when listeners began calling in. Ironically, the imaging of my show was military themed, playing off the *Sarge in the Foxhole* idea. We used sound clips from every military movie we could think of that would fit—from *Stripes* to *Full Metal Jacket* to *Patton* were part of the sound and spirit of my show. Callers were expected to start their call-in with, "Sir, yes, sir!" And they couldn't speak until I gave them permission to, "Speak freely."

It must have resonated with listeners because we went from thirteen affiliates carrying the show to one hundred sixty-eight. But soon after, *Sarge in the Foxhole* was canceled. I didn't take it personally, and in a way, it was a relief. I was working on *Best Damn Sports Show* during the day and the radio show at night. I left the house at nine every morning and didn't get home until almost three the next morning. The fact that I was able to do this for two whole years was a feat unto itself.

I went from making a fortune to losing my radio show, and though I stayed on at *Best Damn* for another couple of months, a new producer took over and soon I was out. I took my leave to go back to being a comedian.

MARITIME VIOLATIONS

When I returned to comedy, I found that something had changed for the better. After two years of working on national network radio, I had gotten used to performing profanity free, and without any prepared material. It had forced me to learn how to be funny without using bad language, tired old bits, or fallback position material. I felt freer on stage than ever before and it occurred to me that even though I had lost some jobs, I had gained mastery over my talent, my mind, and my performances.

My marriage was great and Fiona was working all the time. She was *Snow White* for the Disney live stage show that accompanied the release of *Toy Story*. Clubs around town didn't pay much, and schlepping to comedy clubs for weeks at a time was not lucrative either. So I went back to the ships.

Martin Hall, the head of entertainment at Princess Cruises offered me a two weeks on/two weeks off schedule that enabled me to do what I do but still have a home life. Fiona agreed, so that's what I did to continue supporting us. I'd fly to Mexico on Tuesday, visit on Saturdays when the ship came into Los Angeles for the day, have a conjugal, and go back to the ship until the following Tuesday, when I'd fly home from Mazatlán. Things were going great. We had enough money and plenty of time together at home.

I thought it was the optimal situation.

My wife's sister was getting married in St. Tropez and we were invited to attend. I booked the best hotel in St. Tropez, a five-star place called Hotel Byblos. It was going to cost a fortune but I felt that we were worth it. We flew first class to St. Tropez and attended the wedding. Fiona's sister Sonia was marrying a wealthy banker, whose father was the Canadian Ambassador to France. To give you some idea of the scope of the shindig—the Gypsy Kings were the wedding band. Fiona's father got up to give the Father-of-the-Bride speech and I should have noticed something, because when he got to the part where he was gushing about how happy and proud he was that BOTH of this daughters had found exemplary, talented, smart, loving, faithful, phenomenal men to take care of them and give him grandchildren, my wife was sobbing so uncontrollably that she had to be taken out by her mother and comforted for an hour.

We returned home from France after spending twelve grand on flights, hotel, and the whole shebang. As we entered our apartment, I put down our luggage and Fiona announced that she had fallen in love with someone else. It was like a knife in the heart. My whole body went cold, my heart began to race.

"What do you mean, you've fallen for someone else?"

She repeated what she said.

Couples therapy followed, and a period of working on the marriage, but the sanctity had been broken and the damage was irreparable. I always knew in the back of my mind that the age difference might bite us in the ass but I guess it devoured us. We were done. I procured the services of Bob Campbell, the *Pitbull of Brentwood*, who served her with dissolution of marriage papers the week before Christmas. The marriage had lasted just a shade under five years. I'd have to pay alimony for twenty-seven months, which was one half the length of the union. He advised me to find out from her how much she needed to live on, and add a hundred dollars to that. So that's what I did. We settled—and I set up my online banking auto-pay for the time we agreed upon, and I never looked back.

The pain of the betrayal hurt way more than the cost of the split.

I called my beautiful in-laws, Bronwen and John, to tell them what had happened. I told them that I loved them and retreated to the love and support of people that wouldn't hurt me. David Marciano, Paul Bollen, and Jay Westbrook were my rocks during this time. To a man they each simply told me, "Help her pack." These men advised me that Fiona was on her own journey, and it was my job to love her even though she had acted lovelessly. Looking back, it was the implementation of this critical spiritual tenet that saved my life from lapsing into a deep depression.

It was Christmas week.

The papers were served, but I refused to put Fiona out of our apartment on Christmas, so we spent the very sad holiday together, and that would finish things humanely. I told her to take everything she thought she needed and I gave her a check for first and last month's rent for a new apartment. I had a ship gig coming up and wasn't coming back for two weeks, and I told her to please not be there when I got back.

On Christmas Day, I traveled to my gig on a ship and then on to Florida to attend a men's sober retreat held at a nunnery in Palm Beach. All of the men I knew from my early sober days were in attendance including my brother from another mother David Mitchell, who provided me with my retreat ticket. The first night, a loud, shrill man named Tom M. got up to speak at the podium in front of the two hundred or so gathered. The words he spoke about relationships were clear, but he chose to repeat them five or six times.

"If she ain't got God then you ain't got shit to do with her."

I thought about that.

People who have no higher power or cognizance of such, are usually capable of unconscionable things. My marriage had suffered from that. It was only when one of my pals encouraged me to look at my wife's phone bills did I realize that she had been engaged in an affair for over a year and a half. While I was busting my ass to give her everything that I could give a woman, she was giving herself to another man. Painful, for sure, but easier to understand if I accepted what the speaker kept repeating.

"If she ain't got God, you ain't got shit to do with her."

This spiritual revelation saved me years of rumination and bitterness and enabled me to forgive her for what she'd done, and accept responsibility for picking such a woman to marry. Thank goodness there were no children and thank God for all the very good times.

When we marry we take an oath.

Just because she didn't keep her half of the oath, doesn't mean I ought to go back on my word. In sickness and in health, for richer or poorer, for better or worse. This was sickness, poorer, and worse. I treated her lovingly, fairly, and kept my end of the bargain.

"Help her pack."

"If she ain't got GOD, you ain't got shit to do with her.

The sober men in my life were wise indeed.

The week of the retreat, I ran into a friend from my early sober days who was a builder. He told me he was working on a tract of land out west in Boynton Beach, and that I should go look and see if I liked the model homes. Prior to the end of our marriage, Fiona and I were looking for a house in Los Angeles, but the prices were a million and up. That was too rich for my blood.

Hmmmm, a house in Florida…

Maybe it would be a good investment. The housing market in Florida was going *up, up, up*. I could get a four-bedroom house with a yard and a pool for what my down payment in L.A. would have been.

Even though I was newly single, I had faith that in due time I'd have a family to fill a huge house. I put thirty-two thousand dollars down on a house still under construction and went to sea on another gig. I asked my agent to book me solid while the house was being built so I'd have time to rack up a nice chunk of change to spend on furnishing the new home. I worked exclusively for Princess Cruises at this point and they were good enough to keep me working.

On the first booked cruise of the New Year, only seventeen days after I'd filed for divorce from Fiona, in an elevator on board the Golden Princess, I met a woman named Ania. We nodded and smiled. She was taller than I, it seemed, and beautiful and sexy, but I had a policy against dating the women who worked on board the ships. I was a highly paid entertainer and I'd heard countless stories about situations where entertainers had gotten involved with the ladies and it ended with them losing their job. I maturely decided that the exotic conquest wasn't worth the trouble. And, I'd just been decimated by a relationship that began on board a cruise ship and was costing me dearly—both emotionally and financially—so I wanted to keep my hands in my pockets.

Ania was the shopkeeper of the boutique on board where my CDs and DVDs were sold. I'd periodically go to the shop and check on how sales were going, and each time I did, the rack where they were displayed was empty. That was strange. Entertainer merchandise usually sold better in the lobby right after shows, where the audience members could meet the performers, and get us to autograph their newly purchased CDs and DVDs. I sold thousands of discs this way. But in the ship's boutiques, they usually just sat there amongst the fridge magnets and romance novels.

On Ania's watch, though, they were apparently flying off the shelves. I asked her why my rack was always empty.

"Because I heard you're great," she proclaimed proudly, "And I've been pushing them."

She'd been pushing them. Now that's a teammate. In subsequent days I went back to check again and each time, the rack was empty or only had one left. I kept filling the rack with fresh discs and they kept emptying out. Finally, I felt it was only appropriate that I reward her in some way. I offered her cash and she declined.

"We're not allowed to take money from entertainers."

"Certainly there must be some way I can thank you," I said, "How's about dining with me at one of the restaurants on board? They let you eat don't they?"

She agreed and several nights later we had dinner. It was a wonderful time. I learned that she spoke three languages and that she was from Poland. We had a four-hour dinner. The following week, the actor David Marciano, one of my best friends on Earth was visiting on board with me.

I invited Ania to come to my show if she could and to meet my boy Dave. Apparently they hit it off nicely. After the show, I was outside the theater selling my merchandise and signing autographs, and a gorgeous statuesque blonde stepped behind the table and without saying a word, jumped in and helped me fill in sales chits.

It was Ania. She looked so beautiful out of her ship's uniform I almost didn't recognize her at first. I looked over at her in admiration and gratitude and we just kept working. I thanked her and asked if she'd like to go have a beverage. Since I don't drink, for me that means ginger ale. For her that meant a vodka or two. Have you ever met an eastern European that would say no to a couple of vodkas? I told her I needed to change out of my sweaty show clothes and into something casual and that I needed to go to my cabin.

"I'll go with you," she said simply.

We didn't come out of that cabin until dinner time the next day.

David was supposed to be sharing my cabin, but it was otherwise occupied. He slept that night in one of the public lounges, which is no big deal, because David could fall asleep standing up during a nuclear bomb explosion.

When I got home for a brief stint, I met with my sobriety leadership council—Jere—my sponsor.

"I've met someone," I said.

"Do NOT get involved in anything permanent," he shouted," Until you've finished paying alimony to the last disaster."

Ania and I did get involved, but we didn't make any commitments too quickly. I always tried to do exactly what Jere suggested—it had never led me down the wrong path. As a matter of fact, I've never received bad advice from any of the sober men I've known and listened to over the last twenty-four years.

Do NOT get involved in anything permanent," he shouted," *Until you've finished paying alimony to the last disaster.*

In February, 2007, I made my last alimony payment.

We were on a ship, big shocker, but this time Ania was traveling with me as my guest, not as an employee. I was scheduled for two nights of shows, then I would get off in Grand Cayman and Ania and I would fly to New York, where I was going to do a small part in a movie a dear friend of mine was producing.

I had already bought a ring and I had it with me.

I planned to propose at the Empire State Building *Sleepless in Seattle* style.

I did my second night of shows and while bowing in gratitude for the audience giving me a standing ovation, I bent down and couldn't straighten up. This had happened one other time, when my lower back had seized up. It was agony. I walked off stage doubled over in pain. I couldn't move. I got to the cabin and lay on the bed unable to breathe, afraid of having to go to the bathroom and being unable to get there. I stayed in the same position all night long and we were to leave the next morning. I couldn't move so I called Neil, the ship's nurse, who could administer meds.

"Neil," I said, "I cannot move a muscle."

"Have Ania come and get the miracle bullets," he said.

"Bullet?" I said, "I don't want to kill myself."

Although the pain made me consider it seriously.

Ania came back with some suppositories. *Bullets?* I called the nurse back.

"I don't have hemorrhoids," I said, "I have a bad back."

"Just shove 'em in darling," he said, "You'll be good as new."

I shoved them in and Ania began to pack. I was dictating where stuff should go in the luggage. The only problem with her packing was that THE RING was in my carry-on, and she kept handling my carry-on.

Ania went to put something in the bag and I screamed, "Put that bag down, I'll pack that one!"

She must have thought I was nuts. Then, suddenly, I felt different. My legs bent, I sat up and then stood. *Wow! No pain.* It must have been the butt bullets, because I could walk! We were two hours past our window to get off the ship. On passenger cruise ships, when entering a foreign country, whenever anyone leaves the ship or comes aboard, they must be accompanied by a ship's officer with the appropriate documentation stamped, approved and bureaucratized.

Our appointment that morning was for nine, but it was now eleven thirty. Hoping for the best, Ania and I schlepped the luggage onto the tender boat anyway. (Grand Cayman is a tender port, meaning the ship doesn't dock, it anchors a half-mile off shore and people are tendered to the small dock.) We disembarked the tender and walked up the ramp to enter Grand Cayman. At the top of the ramp there's an immigration booth. A Caymanian official looked at our paperwork.

"Wait! You are in violation!"

"We're just going to the airport," I begged.

"Our customs officer, she is finished for the day. You can't leave. And in trying to do so, you are in violation of maritime law," he kept barking at us, "Princess will be fined forty thousand dollars for each of you!"

Forty grand?! Each?!

While he called some official or other, Ania and I just looked at each other in amazement. All of the elation the suppositories created now that I could straighten up and walk again dissolved into another kind of pain.

"Stand over there and wait!"

Who was coming? The police? Famous Amos? What was happening?

The door of the customs booth burst open and it was a dark-skinned, stern looking woman carrying a backpack. She bantered loudly in island-speak with the guy holding us in custody. Then she climbed up on her stool at her desk.

"You are indeed in violation of maritime codes," she said crisply, "And we are going to fine Princess eighty thousand—"

Before she could finish her sentence, I reached in my bag, got the engagement ring, and went down on one knee.

"Ania," I asked, "Will you please marry me?"

Suddenly the stern lady covered her face with her hands and screamed joyously.

"No, you didn't!" she kept saying, "No, you didn't!"

"Yes," I said to her, "I most certainly did."

Her attention turned to Ania.

"So, girl, will you?" she asked Ania, "Will you?"

Ania laughed her ass off through saying "YES!"

The customs woman instantly turned her attention from the violation of section whatever of maritime law, to the ring.

"Does it fit?" she squealed, "Does it fit?"

It couldn't go past Ania's knuckle.

The customs woman snapped into action, grabbing Ania by the wrist, pulling her along.

"Come on girl," she said, "My bruth-uh works at the jewelry store off Main Street. Come on. We get it sized."

With that, they ran out of the booth, leaving me with the guy who only moments before was holding us in custody. About twenty minutes later they came back and Ania was wearing the ring. The lady got out her inkpad and stamper, opened our passports and stamped them both.

"You have a great life together!" she told us, "Make lots of babies!"

So far we've only made one, but he's the best damn baby you could ever want.

GARRY MARSHALL & MY *BIG BREAK*

It was the fall of 2009. My phone rang. It was Howie Rapp of the Rapp Office, an agency that literally was THE talent agency of the glory days of the Catskills, inviting me to perform in Los Angeles on the *New York Alumni Show*.

For twenty-six years, the *New York Alumni* would do a show in L.A. littered with legends, and honor someone from New York who was huge in show business—Milton Berle, Sid Caesar, and Billy Crystal were past honorees. This year they'd be honoring Lou Gossett, Jr. of Lincoln High in Brooklyn.

"How much?" I asked.

"There's no pay," he said.

Wonderful.

"It would be a great thing for you to do," he begged, "Please consider it seriously."

"Business Class flights roundtrip?"

"No. Coach."

"No way." I was firm. "No pay and coach travel" No thank you."

"I can get you JetBlue extra leg room seats," he offered.

I sighed. "Who else is on this show?"

"It will be awesome," he said, "Sal Richards, Scott Record, Dick Capri, Ben Vereen, Hal Linden, Marilyn Mc Coo and Billy Davis Jr., Cory Kahaney, and a childhood friend of mine, the amazing Broadway baritone William Michals. It'll be great, trust me."

I begrudgingly agreed and flew to L.A.

The show was at the Beverly Hills High School Theater, a thirty-five hundred-seater, that in a few hours would be full. Howie met me there and told me I'd have a twenty minute slot at the end of the show—but because there were so many acts, there'd be no time for me to have a rehearsal. He also told me that Garry Marshall was the master of ceremonies for the evening.

Now you're talking.

Garry Marshall is my favorite of all time—the casino boss in Albert Brooks' *Lost in America,* the author of "Wake Me When It's Funny," the man who singlehandedly put Robin Williams on the map—*Happy Days, Laverne and Shirley, Beaches, Flamingo Kid, Pretty Woman.* THAT Garry Marshall.

Why didn't he tell me that when he offered me the no-pay gig? I'd have paid HIM to be on that show, just for a chance to meet Garry Marshall.

The show began and Garry welcomed the packed theater of show biz savvy New York transplants. I hid in the wings backstage and watched as legendary act after legendary act performed, took their bows and then came backstage to hug Garry and kibitz with him. I stayed way out of the way, because in my mind I wasn't even qualified to breathe the same air as some of these people. Lou Gossett, Jr. and his family were backstage too. Each celebrity act would perform and then be congratulated by even more celebrities—Elliott Gould, Connie Stevens, Shecky Greene—they were all there.

Then I was up.

I remember very little about the set I did. I know I must have gone over time-wise, but at the conclusion of my set, the audience who'd been awesome all night but hadn't yet bestowed a standing ovation to ANY act thus far, gave ME, ME, a thunderous standing ovation. I was overcome with joy, but the larger emotion was relief—relief that I got through it—relief that it went well—relief that I didn't bomb on this cavalcade.

I was aware of one thing during my performance though.

I was aware that Garry Marshall was sitting three rows back from the front on the right in the orchestra seats and he was laughing uproariously at my set, even slapping his legs with his hands throughout. I couldn't think of anything else. I figured, certainly I'd at least get to chitchat with him after my part of the show and exchange pleasantries and shake hands with one of my true comedy idols, but when I went backstage, fresh off the adulation of the sellout crowd, there was no Garry Marshall.

Elliott Gould took my hand.

"You are PHENOMENAL!" he said.

I thanked him for his kind words. Everyone I saw had glowing words of praise for me, but all I was looking for was Garry. The producers of the show were gushing and thanking me. Then a man, who I'd later find out was Norby Walters, the man behind *Night of a Hundred Stars* grabbed me by the arm.

"Someone wants very much to meet you," he said, "Let me bring you over."

I thought, *NOW I get to meet Garry Marshall!* He traipsed me through the sea of show biz VIPs, to a man I didn't recognize. The man was older, well dressed in a sharp suit, with monogrammed shirt cuffs. He was smiling from ear to ear and he grabbed my face with both hands and pulled me in for the biggest kiss.

"I've never seen a comedian that I wouldn't want to follow," he said, "But you are IT! Now get the fuck away from me!"

It was Shecky Greene.

Shecky Greene! A man I'd only laid eyes on in person once at the Playhouse at Grossinger's when I was a little kid.

WOW! Shecky Green loved my set!

This would have been IT on most nights, but I had my heart set on meeting Garry. So after I'd chatted with Shecky for a few minutes, and was introduced to Jerry Vale, and a few others, I was still scanning the backstage area for Garry.

Scott Record, a legendary comedic song and dance man of unmatched stature came over to me and excitedly.

"Do you have an agent here tonight?" he asked, "Garry Marshall absolutely LOVED you."

Now I went looking for the event organizers Fran and Lou

Zigman. I found them chatting off to the side with Lou Gossett, Jr. I asked them where Garry Marshall was.

Fran said, "Oh he had to leave."

I was crushed. "Why did he leave?"

"He had to pee," she said, "And once he went that way he headed to the car."

I asked for his office address so I could send him a note and thank him for watching my set, and tell him that I was sorry I didn't get the chance to shake his hand. She gave me the address and I wrote it down and put it in my pocket.

The next day I flew home and one of the first things I did was write him a letter and I couldn't wait for him to get it so I FedExed it OVERNIGHT. I don't know why I spent twenty bucks to send the man a letter, but I figured an overnight envelope would at least get opened—imagining that a person like Garry gets thousands of letters, communiques, scripts, or what have you—so I sent the letter expensively and forgot about it.

That was Thursday.

By the time the weekend went by, I'd forgotten about sending the letter. The following Wednesday evening, on the night I meet weekly with a bunch of men in recovery that I sponsor, we were starting our meeting with seven minutes of meditation and my phone rang.

Damn! I ALWAYS turn my phone off during meetings.

I looked down at my phone, and the screen read "BLOCKED." Well, I only have one person in my life whose number is blocked when he calls, and that's my friend Rich Taite.

I answered the phone, whispering, "What the fuck do you want?"

"What the fuck do I want?" I didn't recognize the voice on the other end immediately.

"Rich?" I asked.

"I do alright for myself." The voice sounded familiar but now I knew it certainly wasn't my pal Rich. I have friends who do impressions and it sounded like someone doing an impression of a Jewish man.

I kept saying, "Who is this? Where are you from?"

"I'm from the Bronx."

"Okay," I said, "You're from the Bronx. Where in the Bronx?"

"DeWitt Clinton High School."

"Okay," I said again. "But I don't know anybody from DeWitt Clinton High School."

"This is Garry Marchiarelli," he said.

He was toying with me. Only then, after about three minutes on the phone, did I finally realize who was on the other end.

"Mr. Marshall?" I asked meekly.

"That's right, you moron." He said, "*What the fuck do I want?* Who answers a phone that way?"

"A moron like me, I guess," I said, "I am sooooooo sorry."

"I'm beginning to realize that," he said. "I got your note and I was going to write you back, but nobody writes notes anymore, so I thought I'd call you. So—how are you, Mr. Sarge?"

All I could do was keep apologizing for my initial rudeness. He assured me that it was okay—and then the bombshell.

"Listen, I watched you the other night and not since I first saw Robin have I seen a comedian demolish a crowd like you did," he said. "I'd like you to come to New York. I'm doing a little movie and I've written a part for you in it. Would you come?"

"Would I come to New York to be in your movie?"

"On second thought, don't come. I'll BRING you. If you come it'll cost you money, if I BRING you then you'll be brought and it'll be on me, how does that sound?"

"Yyyyyyyessss, that sounds great, Mr. Marshall, sir."

"Garry," he said, "Call me Garry."

"Right, right" I said, "Garry."

"So I have your number now," he said, "I'll call you, and we'll bring you, and when are you coming to L.A.?"

"Next week," I said, "Next week."

"Great!" he said. "Call me and we'll have a nice lunch at the club and we'll talk about your role in the movie."

I didn't even think to ask what movie it was but the following week someone called me from his office to get my address and the very next day I received the script pages for the holiday blockbuster *New Year's Eve*. I arrived in New York and stayed in a residence hotel in the Times Square area.

I had seven scenes with dialogue.

Garry cast me as *Monty,* the confidante and bodyguard to Jon Bon Jovi's character, *Jensen,* a busy, love-struck rock star. Not much of a stretch for Jon—though he's not your average rock star. Jon has been with the same woman for decades, has a bunch of kids he's in love with, and makes a life out of doing the music business as a passion and a business, not as his personal opportunity to bang groupies. Several times I had the privilege of hanging in his trailer. My trailer was a sliver, like a bookshelf for a human, Jon's was movie star phenomenal, with a full kitchen, queen-size bed, and a full entertainment system. He invited me in and we talked about life, our kids and being from New York. He generously would receive people who popped by for autographs or just wanted to see him in person.

I was in New York on the *New Year's Eve* shoot for over a month, and in that time had several encounters with some of the twenty-five stars who were doing their various days on the film. I didn't have tons to do, but when I did, I was amazed at how much easier preparing for a few lines on camera was compared to entertaining fifteen hundred people live. I'd give anything to do more of the movie stuff and if it's meant to be, it will be. In the meantime, I relished EVERY MINUTE of being there and it was only made easier around the work that everyone knew I'd been handpicked by Garry. I was his guy. That afforded me a level of treatment and respect on par with the other veteran people on the film.

Garry's people are wonderful. We were shooting in twenty degree New York winter conditions, and it might as well have been the Caribbean with all of the humor and warmth flowing around. I was allowed to watch everything that was being shot from *the video village*, a little area where the director and script supervisor and producers congregate to watch the work being done. Here I was an actor with a small part, and not once was I asked to get out of the way or make myself scarce. A Garry Marshall set is populated with people who are glad to be working with him, and he returns the favor by making every person feel special. He never misses a chance to ask people how they're doing, or if they need anything, or if he can do anything for them. It's beautiful.

The first day of shooting, we were on a soundstage shooting Bon Jovi tour bus stuff at Kauffman-Astoria studios and I was supposed to enter the bus with Katherine Heigl and deliver a couple of lines to her and Jon. We did the scene about eight times—not a lot for a big budget movie. After Garry shouted *cut, print, check the gate*, which means we'd be moving on to shoot something else, he appeared from out of nowhere, took me aside and handed me a dollar.

"Do you have a pen?" he asked.

I went over to a table, got one, and he signed the dollar and gave it to me.

"This is your first perfect close-up dollar," he said, "It takes some people four movies to get one of these, and you got yours on the FIRST SCENE."

I was thrilled.

"Don't spend the dollar," he said, "You might need it someday.

I have that dollar framed and in the entrance way to my house. It is one of my most cherished possessions to this day.

I don't think Garry Marshall really knows or cares what his impact has been in my life. Putting me in the movie, yeah, that's fantastic. But his approval of me as a comedian and comedic actor has given me the confidence to pursue opportunities that I'd never attempted. Being asked to be his catcher in the parking lot of his office while he warmed up his arm for his Thursday softball. Coming in to his office, having him tell Heather, *Hold my calls, I'm in here with Sarge.* Random calls from him on my birthday to wish me a "great day." For a man like him to validate me as a comedian and as a man is life changing. This is a guy who wrote for Jack Paar on the original *Tonight Show!* He wrote for Joey Bishop, Lucy, Dick Van Dyke, Robin Williams, and countless others. The way he opens himself to me has made every trip I've made to L.A. incomplete unless we've had lunch or spent some time telling stories. The amazing thing is he always wants to know about ME, as though nothing he's doing is particularly interesting enough to waste my time with.

What a MENSCH.

The movie wrapped in April of 2011 and would be premiering in December. Unbeknownst to me, most of my scenes were cut for private reasons Garry shared with me in a letter he sent to my post office box mailing address. I won't share what he told me, but suffice to say that for once, a disappointment really wasn't personal—he assured me that my work had been wonderful and that he would hire me again.

But as luck would have it, I don't check that box very often and I didn't receive that letter until AFTER I'd returned from the movie premiere held at Grauman's Chinese Theatre in Hollywood. When I arrived at the premiere, as far as I knew, my scenes were still in. The day after the first screening for the studio I had received a call from one of the writers who told me that I got six big laughs at the screening and that this was my big break. So I was excited. When it was time to go to the premiere, I showed up and walked the red carpet with all of the other stars in attendance. Garry stopped to spend some time taking pictures with me in front of the paparazzi. He'd sent the letter weeks ago and assumed I'd received it and kept thanking me for coming. I wouldn't know why he kept thanking me until I sat in the theater next to Jim Belushi and watched the film, only to find very little of me in the final version we were watching. To be fair, some huge stars also had only one or two scenes. When the credits rolled, I think I saw my name scroll by, but I felt like I'd been kicked in the stomach by a dozen kangaroos. Remember, last I heard I was hilarious in the movie. I wouldn't get the letter until I returned home to Florida. In it, he explained that he had to make room on the screen for a parade of big name stars, but nothing could diminish how funny my scenes were and how hard he fought to keep them in the final cut. So, even though some of the stuff didn't make the movie, "your friends will still be able to see you there." I can't say I would have walked the red carpet and rushed to Hollywood for the opening had I received the letter before I left, but, in retrospect, the whole experience was a gift from one of the most generous people I know.

I am grateful to know Garry Marshall. And I will love him forever for being one of the only people, other than my Poppy Herman, who extended himself to me, made me a promise, and kept it.

Rare indeed.

A BOY WITHOUT SKIN

On September 19, 2008, I delivered Zander Jacob Pickman.

I never thought I would be given that honor—of being a father.

Ania broke her water and we had prepared everything you could in advance. Bags packed, *check*. Extra pillows for Mommy, *check*. A battery operated fan, *check*. We jumped in the car and raced over to Boca Community Hospital for the birth of our son. We knew we were having a boy, so, seven months of sleeping on her back were over for my wife, who's always liked to sleep face down.

We glided into the suite ready to go. Our Ob-Gyn was a Chinese woman named Dr. Xiao Mei Zeng. I joked for the months leading up to our big event that since her name is pronounced Show-me, that she should change her last name to Your-vagina.

After twelve hours in labor the time had come. Dr. Xiao Mei arrived and took control. She was in a lab coat, plastic welding helmet and was wearing what looked like oven mitts. I was watching through a window. She put my wife's feet in the stirrups. One ankle in Atlanta and the other in Toronto and the baby would be coming from the valley of West Vaginnia. It was game on. She motioned for me.

"Come inside, come inside."

I poked my head in the doorway.

"I already did, that's why we hired you."

"Don't be silly," she said, "Let's go get in here and deliver your son, it's a big honor."

The nurses came into the hall and brought me a smock and welder's shield and mitts of my own. I came in and the doctor immediately began shouting at me.

"He wants to come out! Go and get him!"

After a dozen deep breaths and pushes from my wife, the head came and my hands were right there. The doctor told Ania to push, and as she winced and breathed deeply, the rest of my son came out directly out of West Vaginnia and into my waiting hands.

I held him tenuously at first.

Zander Jacob Pickman was seven pounds, thirteen ounces. I'd gained seven and a half pounds many times in my life, but never before had I been this happy about it.

Dr. Zeng handed me a pair of scissors.

"Go ahead!"

"Are you kidding," I said, "We have a moyl coming Tuesday."

"Not THAT!" she yelled. "CUT THE CORD, CUT THE CORD!"

"It's still plugged into my wife!" I yelled, "I'm not cutting a cord that's still plugged in."

Zander is six now, and I haven't been back to West Vaginnia since.

By now *The Delivery Story* is a staple in my show. But my son has given me much, much more than comedy material.

From the time he was born he had great difficulty around feedings. My wife was breast feeding and he was always crying. Not just *I'm hungry* crying but *I'm in agony* crying. We'd later find out that he was highly allergic to milk and beef, both major components of my wife's diet. By the time Ania had eliminated those foods, it was too late. The poor thing had already associated pain and systemic discomfort with feeding. He made the transition from Mommy to bottles okay, but he wouldn't make the transition to regular food until his first cracker when he was four years-old.

We knew something was terribly wrong, but got no solace from our pediatrician. We went to specialists and learned of no concrete solutions. Zander was unhappy mostly all of the time. As an infant and then as a toddler, he'd scrape the salt off of pretzel rods, but other than that, no food would be consumed except puree of soy mango yogurt. Five times a day, my wife would feed him soy yogurt, and it had to be mango, and it had to be white. Ania would load the yogurt up with mineral and vitamin supplements, so he was getting nutrition, but Zander absolutely would not eat.

At eighteen months, we were absolutely at our wit's end.

We had therapists coming to the house working to desensitize his relationship with food, and we'd make frequent office visits, but it was only getting worse.

One of the therapists led us to go online and look at a program in Baltimore at Johns-Hopkins called the Kennedy-Krieger Institute. They specialize in feeding children with developmental difficulties. After many questionnaires and phone interviews, we hoped this would be the help we needed. Desperate and terrified, we flew to Baltimore and were evaluated by a multi-disciplinary team of doctors at Kennedy-Krieger. The evaluation was expensive so we could just imagine what the out of pocket would be should we be accepted into the program. However, we finally had a definitive answer.

Our son suffered from moderate to extreme Sensory Processing Disorder, or SPD.

Much of my life I couldn't stop eating.

My son couldn't start.

Yet we are exactly the same, in that we were both born hyper-sensitive—as if without skin. My reaction to that sensitivity was to try to escape what hurt too much through drugs and alcohol. His reaction was try to escape being *attacked* by tactile sensations by refusing to eat.

Kennedy-Krieger had a process that basically boiled down to force feeding. Ania had seen videos online of their methods and wasn't happy about it. Plus, many of the kids at the Institute were severely compromised physically, emotionally, and behaviorally. Zander seemed like the least challenged of all the kids we saw while we were there.

We also didn't have the THREE HUNDRED THOUSAND DOLLARS it would take to enter the treatment cycle.

So we waited, and worried, unsure what to do next.

Then out of the blue, it turned out that my cousin, Cathy Levine, also had a son with SPD. They had spent some time at a place in Colorado that actually helped him.

Ania, a tireless internet researcher and Mommy with Challenges group member, looked into the place my cousin went with her son—the STAR Center in Denver, Colorado. (STAR stands for *Sensory Therapy And Research*.) Ania did her due diligence on the place, and liked what she saw—so she arranged for us to go to the STAR Center for a ten week program. That would mean we'd have to move ourselves lock, stock and barrel to Denver. They have affiliated housing in town homes near the center, so we loaded up the car, shipped it to Denver and flew ahead of it to get the help we hoped would make a difference.

From the day we arrived and were evaluated, we knew we were home. The specialists, therapists and handlers headed up by Dr. Lucy Miller knew their stuff. Dr. Lucy had been part of the autism movement and determined that all autistic children had SPD, but all kids with SPD were not autistic. Zander fell into the latter class.

In addition to Dr. Lucy, STAR had a team of world class professionals. Dr. Kay Toomey is on property and is world renowned in her revolutionary S.O.S feeding protocol. They also worked with a developmental pediatrician, a nutritionist, two occupational therapists, and a psychiatrist.

They ALL worked together as a team to help our Zander with his difficulty—and help they did. Their method is to train the whole family to reconfigure their household to engage the child in the necessary therapy. They literally teach you a new way of interacting with your child. The work is endless and continuous, long after you leave the STAR Center.

A couple of weeks into our course of treatment, which was two hours in the morning and two hours in the afternoon, six days a week for ten weeks, I asked to see Dr. Lucy. I entered her office and we sat knee to knee. I thanked her because since we'd been there, my son was making amazing strides and it had only been two weeks. I was amazed and convinced that whatever they were doing was working. I asked the doctor if she had any show biz types raising money for the center, which incidentally is a non-profit. No one was.

I told her I would do anything in my power to help on her mission to help as many kids and families suffering from what we were for the remainder of my life. I was that impressed and motivated with the work that we were doing in Denver.

Zander was getting better.

That's all that mattered.

When your child is ill, your heart hurts. We empathize with parents of kids with even more serious illnesses and count ourselves amongst the lucky.

When we arrived at STAR, Zander was a feeding tube candidate. Getting him nourishment was that difficult. Now, some four years later, he has advanced and flourished and triumphed entirely because of the work that began at STAR and the work that continued with STAR-trained therapists when we returned to Florida.

I have learned more from being a Dad then Zander will ever understand. From the moment he was born, I have experienced an immense love that only grows deeper and more important.

After years of being in show business, now I do what I do for my son. Every show, every appearance, every deed I do, I do for him. He has no idea how much more patient and charitable I've become since his birth.

My son will never see me drunk or high and that's a daily thing.

I didn't think I'd make thirty years-old and here I am, a middle-aged guy with a six year-old. I am grateful for his presence in my life because every decision I make, I filter through the same question.

"Will this be good for our family?"

The universe has seen fit to give us only as much challenge as we can handle, and because of my amazing, dedicated, intelligent and creative wife, Ania, we have triumphed. She carried him in her body, and freshly prepared every meal that he refused to eat for years. She got up with him and stayed up with him night after sleepless night trying to soothe our baby because he didn't want Daddy, he wanted his Mommy. Even surviving that paternal injustice was transformational because it taught me to put myself aside and love him even when he loved only his Mommy.

One day, God-willing a long, long time from now, I won't be around anymore. The reason I wrote this book, is to make sure that my Zander knows in his heart and in his mind and in HIS book, from his Dad, that everything I did in my life was to give him the very best I have to offer. My difficulties taught me to always do my best. I'm so grateful to have survived my personal challenges, to have done the things I've done, and to have been to the places I've been.

Because of my son, it has all been FOR SOMETHING.

Hopefully, because of this book, my son will always know how very much I love him.

I always have and I always will.

As a matter of fact, I love each and every one of you who read this—because if I love YOU, it means I love ME—and that's the diametric opposite of who I used to be.

Thank God.

A TRIBUTE TO GARRY K. MARSHALL

Friendship isn't about who you've known the longest. It's about who walks into your life and says, "I'm here for you," and proves it. Garry K. Marshall was such a friend to me.

When we met seven years ago, I'm sure he didn't need another friend in his life. This was a man who was always surrounded by those who loved him. He was a husband, a grandfather, a father, a brother, and a boss who cared deeply about people; a man who was never too busy to be there when it mattered.

He was a brilliant talent, who spent a lifetime making comedians shine with his joke writing, turning starving actors into stars with his vision and imagination, and making billions of dollars for television networks and film studios with his inspired creativity, and with his own brand of humor, infused with love and hope.

Garry walked into my life on October 2, 2010. He was the master of ceremonies for a show in Beverly Hills—a last-minute gig I almost turned down since it was a charity event, and on that night, at that moment, I was thinking, Maybe I do enough for charity already… Thank God I decided to show up. Because that night a door opened, and once it opened, it never closed.

Just knowing Garry was there blew my mind. He was a legend. He had touched the careers of giants like Jack Paar, Danny Thomas, Joey Bishop, Dick Van Dyke, Lucille Ball, Bette Midler, Jackie Gleason even… and he personally discovered Robin Williams. Make no mistake, what he might think about my act mattered to me. If I could make a guy like him laugh, maybe I could do anything.

I did a 30-minute set. Before the sweat had dried from my performance, Scott Record, an amazing song and dance man in his own right, rushed to my side backstage telling me he had watched my act sitting beside Garry, and that Garry wasn't just laughing—he was slapping his legs and guffawing while tears rolled down his face.

In terms of feeling good about my work, knowing I made such a man laugh like that would have been enough. Dayenu. And initially it looked like it would have to be enough, since when I asked Scott if he could introduce me to Mr. Marshall, if I could just meet the man and shake his hand, Scott said Garry was gone. He'd had to pee, and since the bathroom was on the way to the parking lot, he'd just kept going.

My heart sank. But I asked the producers of the event, Lou and Fran Zigman, for Garry's address. The moment I got home I penned him a letter and sent it overnight to his Burbank offices. I wanted him to know how much it meant to me that he was there, and how much a respect and admire him.

A week later I got a call from an "Unknown" number. "Who is this?" I barked into the phone, thinking it was a telemarketer. "I'm from the Bronx," said someone with one of the most distinctive New York accents on the planet. "I'm a DeWitt Clinton graduate." How much of an idiot was I, that I still didn't recognize that voice. And now I was annoyed. I snapped back, "I don't know anyone from the Bronx or DeWitt Clinton High School." He offered another piece of info, "It's Garry Mosh-A-Relli. Everyone thinks I'm Jewish, but I'm Italian."

Honestly, how stupid am I that I still didn't have a clue. "It's Garry Marshall, you shmuck. You wrote me a note, didn't you?"

I was beyond embarrassed, beyond horrified. "I am sooooo sorry, sir," I stammered.

"I'm starting to get that about you," he quipped.

But what came out of his mouth next was the most empowering, inspirational, motivational piece of feedback I'd ever receive. "I saw you perform the other night," he said, "And I've seen everybody. You reminded me of the first time I saw Robin Williams. I had the same reaction to you. You are a perfect blend of character, brilliant performing chops and genius and I want to invite you to New York to work on a little picture I'm doing, I've written a part for you. Will you come?"

I couldn't speak. All that would come out was stuttering. "Uhhhhhh, yes, thank you, uhhhhhh of course, really, thank you." As soon as I got the words out, he went on to say, "You know what, don't come to New York."

"Don't come to New York?!"

"No, don't come," he said, "You'll be brought. I'll bring you to New York."

I was still a tongue-tied mess, only able to parrot back what he said. "Don't come, I'll be brought?"

"That's right," he said, "I'll bring you. Being brought is better than coming, because if you come YOU have to pay and if I bring you, I'M paying."

So he brought me. And my world changed. From the night in 2010, when he saw me perform, to the day we lost him, July 19, 2016, Garry Marshall was my friend and made me feel like part of his family. Every phone call, every two and a half hour lunch in his office where he'd tell his beloved, phenomenal personal assistant Heather Hall, "Hold my calls, Sarge is here!" Then he'd grin. "Nobody calls anymore, I just like saying that.".

Not true.

The world called Garry Marshall. From memorial statements of folks like Henry Winkler and Julia Roberts, the common theme was a feeling I'd experienced myself: His love. Garry made everyone feel like they were close to him and that he loved them. No matter how big the star, when in his presence, his loving persona shone even brighter and erased any vestige of ego or pettiness.

Garry's humility and self-deprecating quips were ever-present. But his smile, we all know his smile.

The heartfelt smile that made global warming seem like an ice age. He always made me feel like "a somebody." His position in the world made his opinion of my comedy matter. His position in my life, made me feel like I matter.

His dignity dignified me. And as it turned out, he basically scripted out my whole life for me:

My wife Ania is my "Pretty Woman."

I live in Florida, the home of some of the most beautiful "Beaches" in the world.

Almost all of my days are "Happy Days."

A black Jew and an Italian guy that everyone thinks is Jewish walk into a deli... Truly an "Odd Couple."

Mr. Maschiarelli, I think of you every day. I will always love you.

Made in the USA
Columbia, SC
02 October 2020